REFLECTIONS ON GROWING OLD

JOHN LAFARGE, S.J.

Reflections on Growing Old

LOYOLA UNIVERSITY PRESS

CHICAGO 60657

Imprimi Potest:
Timothy A. Curtin, s.j.
Socius, New York Province, Society of Jesus
September 29, 1962

Nihil obstat:
Daniel V. Flynn, j.c.d.
Censor Librorum

Imprimatur:
✠Francis Cardinal Spellman
Archbishop of New York
April 20, 1963

ISBN 0–8294–0191–1

TO

JIM LAWRENCE, JOE O'GORMAN, BILL REID,

AND OTHER HONORED SURVIVORS OF H.C. '01,

THE FIRST CLASS OF THE CENTURY.

ACKNOWLEDGMENTS

Special acknowledgment is due to Rabbi Seymour Siegel, assistant professor of theology at the Jewish Theological Seminary, New York City, for the references to Jewish teaching on the dignity of old age; also to Reverend Hugh J. Bihler, s.j., professor of experimental psychology at Loyola Seminary, Shrub Oak, N.Y., for quotations from St. Augustine.

CONTENTS

INTRODUCTION

In 1961 I published an article in *America* magazine, which later appeared in brochure form, entitled "On Turning Seventy." It proposed the idea of regarding one's old age as a great enterprise — standing on its own merits — not just a mere calamity which you bewail, or just a misfortune to which you cannot be resigned. It didn't prescribe one or the other of the various ways by which you can, or are supposed to be able to, cheat old age. You know the kind of thing I mean: diving into icy water at the age of eighty, or enrolling for graduate study at some respectable university in your declining years. No, it merely suggested that after all old age has its own meaning, like other phases of human life, and that the wisest thing we could do, when age crept up on us, would be to explore that meaning and to adopt some general plan of action, so as really to profit by it.

The little article met a surprisingly favorable reception. Pretty nearly everybody who read it, and made some sort of a comment, liked the idea, and for some reason seemed to find the proposition quite original. This wealth of responses seemed to bring out a curious paradox, if I may use the word. On the one hand, nobody is ready to show much interest in old age. Its problems are unpleasant areas of our life, which we would more happily forget. Indeed it is said that of all peoples, presumably "cultured" and intelligent peoples, we Americans pay the least honor to old age as a natural phase of life. Perhaps that is true. Color prints of elderly people are seldom used as come-ons for the latest brand of cigarettes or aspirin tablets. On the other hand, if you delve a little more deeply, you find that in reality people are much more concerned about age than you would imagine. We would rather not talk about it, but yet, if someone has something really worth while to say on this unpopular subject, we are anxious to hear. It's not just the facts that people would like to ascertain — indeed so many of these facts are distressingly evident — but particularly they want to know the *meaning* of the facts. What is the explanation of this universal phenomenon, in terms of ordinary human values? Is age somehow or other an insult to my humanness?

People are interested in the question of old age for the simple reason that one of these days they too are going to get that way. And they wonder how our civilization is going to accommodate this ever-increasing proportion of oldsters. More and more of your friends and acquaintances will live serenely to be eighty or eighty-five, and it can happen to you. Yet there is also a desire to resolve the old-age problem in some sort of rational terms. "The problem can never be solved in a spirit of moral and religious relativism."[1]

[1] Emil L. Fackenheim, *Commentary*, May 10, 1962, p. 402.

Introduction

Some who commented on my article disagreed with my manner of approaching the subject. They felt I should have dwelt more upon the social injustices that so many aged people suffer, and not devote my time to studying what age itself has to offer. However, such a treatment, most worthy in itself, would have distracted me from what I wished to say. My aim was to make some positive remarks upon the genuine values of old age. The considerations put forth on the following pages attempt to present just such a positive view: to explore what old age has to say to us, in the light of our faith, in the light of our personal experience. It is an attempt to answer the very obvious question: what is the *necessity* of our present exile, suffering, deprivation, humiliation, and, eventually, death?

Let me express briefly the idea from which this little book was written. It states a personal view, born of experience and faith.

I believe that old age is a gift, a very precious gift, not a calamity. Since it is a gift, I thank God for it daily.

Age robs us and enriches us. It robs us of life, as we know life and love it; to a certain extent it *diminishes* us. It separates us from loved ones and much human living and makes us dependent upon others. Yet it offers great and subtle compensations: many insights, often much peace, and certain fruits of wisdom. It brings new contributions, new hopes, fulfillments, perspectives, especially for the thoughtful. Old age does mean a diminishment, and always ends in that utter diminishment, which is death. Yet through diminishment age brings us a new life: a life

that flows directly from the source of all life and youth—
the Eternal.

This new life, the life of the Resurrection, is nourished
within us here and now, in the struggles of this world. It is
nourished in us by the operation of the Holy Spirit: a
continual life-building, which becomes more intense as we
advance in years and in diminishment. The increase of this
life is the fulfillment of God's promises: it is God's *Amen*.
His Amen, His steadfast love for us, in the language of the
Bible, is the basis of our hope.

I can reject this divine operation by bitterness, cowardice,
and complaint. Or I can accept it by thanksgiving: by faith,
hope, and love.

Growth-through-diminishment is not some arbitrary formula. Rather it is in accord with an archetype that runs
through all nature, through the evolution of physical life,
through the evolution of man's cultural life as well. And
it is in accord with what inspired history tells us of God's
ways of dealing with the human race, and is proclaimed by
the Saviour of mankind a law of the Kingdom.

This new life takes the form of love: of a dynamic,
tangible force in human affairs. A reward of old age is to
give to me ever new and varied opportunities for the experience of this new life of love for God and man. The
acceptance of these new opportunities, as they present
themselves to me each day, is an Amen of joy. It is also
an Amen of atonement, of reparation, for my own sins and
for those of others, in union with the divine sacrifice offered
by the Son of God. The immense dynamic force of love —
so easily forgotten, or else misrepresented or caricatured in

our times — is the force of love's *dimensions,* seen in the variety and richness of their application to each individual, and to society.

Love, therefore, means responsibility: of society toward the aged, and of the aged toward one another and toward society. Love also demands courage: the courage to walk bravely in co-operation with the Holy Spirit, the courage to make the complete and final offering of our lives.

The five parts of these considerations, *Growth-through-Diminishment, Our Steadfast Hope, The Power of Love, Society's Responsibility,* and *Courage in Old Age,* explain these ideas in more detail in the rest of the book.

REFLECTIONS ON GROWING OLD

Part I

GROWTH-THROUGH-DIMINISHMENT

When you live from out of the nineteenth century and deep into the twentieth, you cannot fail to be impressed by the great number of conveniences the present epoch provides for those who survive into it, and who enjoy the financial competence to make use of them. The present generation of aged are the beneficiaries of an incredible advance in the development of medical care and social organization. In the field of travel alone they enjoy now a multitude of comforts.

Yet you cannot even today travel intelligently without confronting a distressing quota of human misery, stark old-age misery, in our enormously progressive and progressing period. Even where such misery does not exist, where old age enjoys our mid-century comforts and conveniences, the facts of old age, as such, still remain.

We cannot change the fundamental facts. They meet you at every turn. You may bitterly oppose the coming of old age: try to ignore it, conceal it, resist it by every means possible. For a time you may achieve some degree of success with the aid of wigs or vitamins. Yet time and age are inexorable. Even Methuselah had to capitulate in the end. But we *can* determine our own attitude toward this phenomenon, and it is of the utmost importance that we make such a determination. Is the old-age phenomenon an impenetrable negative, as far as I personally am concerned, or is it but the negative preliminary to a final transformation of my existence?

If the disasters of old age were a merely casual or morbid affair, you might say: best forget it! You can't "do" anything about it, and you only add to your troubles by dwelling upon them, like a person who is afflicted with some unpleasant physical deformity. The affliction, in this philosophy, is not pleasant, it is simply a fact which you stoically try to endure as best you can, and you hope, by this or that scheme or device, to make some kind of truce or bargain with it as long as you exist.

But old age is not just a casual calamity. On the contrary, it is a natural phase of our human life that stands in its own right, just as does every other human life-phase: infancy, childhood, youth, adulthood. It enjoys its own dignity, its own privileges and character. The testimony of thinkers of all times refuses to consider old age as a quite meaningless misfortune, a mere derogation from normal youthfulness. Such might have been the mentality of very primitive man, for whom the elders were no longer useful as hunters and providers of the tribal sustenance. When the old warrior couldn't hurl any more flint-tipped javelins, it was time to do away with him, taking care of course that his ghost didn't return of nights and make trouble. Yet even with the primitives, aged people enjoyed mysterious powers of magical might and counsel. Certainly if any degree of civilization exists, the testimony of thinkers insists upon honoring old age, and gives it a special place and significance. At nearly every turn in the long cultural road we find old age loved and cherished. The Greeks, who saw such transcendent significance in youth and beauty, found beauty, too, in old age: the dignity of elders. Elegantly garrulous Cicero (he admits this weakness) has all sorts of nice things to say about old age as it appears to a successful statesman and a gentleman farmer, though he must have appeared rather unconvincing to the employees on his carefully tended estates. Cicero bears a splendid testimony to the grand old Roman tradition of honor to senior citizens: the reverence with which they were listened to, in public and in private, the dignity of their public appearance, a dignity reflected in the stately tradition of our modern court procedure and the prerogatives of our assembled legislators. The very word senate, *senatus*, implies the honorable position conferred by tradition and law upon the aged.

From the Book of Genesis on, the Bible unrolls a perspective of aged dignitaries: the political wisdom of the (woefully ignored) elderly counselors of the youthful King Rehoboam, the aged mother of Samuel; the heroic nonagenarian Eleazar in the time of the Maccabees, who preferred to be "sent to hell" rather than to eat forbidden food; the prophetic souls, Anna and Simeon, who welcomed the child Jesus in the Temple, etc. And this dignity is upheld, in spite of an ever-present consciousness of the shortness, the uncertainty of man's temporal condition: "Thou dost sweep men away; they are like a dream, like grass which is renewed in the morning: in the morning it flourishes and is renewed; in the evening it withers" (Psalm 90[89]:5, 6).

Biblical and rabbinical literature offer an impressive array of testimonials to the intrinsic dignity of old age: "Thou shalt rise up before the hoary head, and honor the face of the old, and fear thy God: I am the Eternal" (Leviticus 19:32). "The hoary head is a crown of glory; it is found in the way of righteousness" (Proverbs 6:31). "The glory of young men is their strength; and the beauty of old men is the hoary head" (Proverbs 20:29). "Hearken unto thy father that begot thee, and despise not thy mother when she is old" (Proverbs 23:22). "He who welcomes an old man is as if he welcomed the Shechinah [the Divine Presence]" (Gen. R., Toledot, LXIII, 6 fin. 9th. p. 684), etc.

Rabbi Jose bar Jehudah of Chephar ha-Babli said: "He who learns from the young to what is he like? To one who eats unripe grapes and drinks wine from his wine-press. And he who learns from the old to what is he like? To one who eats ripe grapes and drinks old wine" (Pirke Aboth, IV, 26).

All these considerations point vividly to the fact that in the normal, unperturbed view of the whole of human life, old age enjoys a special meaning. Childhood has its own significance, so has early youth, adolescence, young adulthood, and middle age. Each stage of our life merits its own prerogatives and is best judged by its own standards, not simply in the terms of what has preceded or what follows after. So many human abnormalities come from trying to act outside of one's own age: the child who is never really a child, but starts trying to be an adolescent when hardly out of kindergarten; the youth who tries to put on the authority of a grown man or woman; the elderly person who apes the young.

If old age is a normal phase of our life, why then can we not integrate it into our whole scheme? Why can we not search for its deeper meaning?

The more meaning you have found in life, the clearer will be the meaning of old age. If life were static, if we never changed, if life were like the surface of the moon, we would have antiquity, yes — we would be chronologically old. But we would not grow old in the human sense. The moon is ancient enough, but it is not venerable, in the sense that an elderly human being is venerable. The earth's satellite has just continued to be, and that is all, something like the two-century-old turtle that was found in the Galapagos Islands. I am interested in the ancient turtle as a curious phenomenon, and I pay the old fellow a certain respect. He is, in a sense, a cultural treasure. Yet he does not spell out for me the richness of life, as does the ancient human being. No publisher will be interested in the turtle's autobiography. The reptile's simple doings at the age of six months are pretty much the same as those which occupy him at the age of 175.

The turtle does not inquire into the meaning of his own survival. He does not, to our knowledge, inquire into the meaning of anything except as it may affect his immediate comfort and elementary wants. I can conceive a human being living like a turtle, with no thought either to the past or the morrow, but most of us are made of other stuff

[25]

and want to know — for our own and for our children's sake — what all this body-and-soul-shaking phenomenon signifies.

We are only defeating ourselves, therefore, if we look upon the state of age as something quite meaningless, if we see it as a mere misfortune, if its anticipation is something we would gladly banish from our minds. Today, when we live in an image-controlled world, the question is paramount. Is my picture of old age something I would willingly ignore if it were in any way possible? Or do I see it as a cherished image, one that I like to dwell upon, something that grows richer in profound human meaning, as I penetrate it more deeply?

The great fact of old age, no matter how you look at it, is diminishment in one form or another. So the question recurs: why is life as I now know it, as it affects me in my present existence, such a curiously diminishing thing? Why must I change so much? Why must I grow weak, why do I have to resign from occupations? Why do I find myself becoming confused, forgetting names and misaddressing envelopes? What, on the other hand, is the meaning of so many of the finer things of my latter existence? Why do I clearly see now many perspectives and relationships that carried no patent meaning for me in earlier days?

If you are of the sociable type, you suffer from seeing and conversing with fewer people. Old acquaintances have a way of dying off when you least expect it, indeed you didn't even realize that they, too, have been growing old. Though the wise have philosophized on these sudden absences ever since Heraclitus lost his dear old Carian guest, the obits let you down when they happen to you personally and sometimes are a bitter blow. Your outer circle is narrowed, and internally you are in poorer shape to cope with the changing world around you.

Is this all merely unintelligible fate, or is there some reason to it? I do not find the answer to this question in a certain type of simplified religiosity, which says: "Forget the present! All will be taken care of later in a new and glorious world. Be content with short rations in this life, in view of the good things to come. Fulfill the obligations of your code, religious and moral — this is necessary for winning the great bet of the afterlife. The rest of the time you can spend on being a good citizen in any way you find convenient. An hour or two Sunday morning should suffice to keep you straight on this afterlife business. There is so much to do the rest of the time."

This exhortation has a familiar sound. It suggests a certain type of religious preachment, which is full of truth and cogency, yet does not wholly satisfy. "The present, as you say, is a time of mixed joy and sorrow. But cheer up, better times are coming. This trouble will soon be over and in the future life I have permanent happiness prepared for you. Don't attach too much importance to the present: the present will soon fade. The future is everlasting. All that happens now is contingent, as the philosophers say. It has no great meaning, except as a kind of test, to make sure you select the correct answer."

But if only the future contains the key to my existence, why should I be concerned about what happens to me at the present time? Certainly, by commitment to my future

[27]

salvation, I have opted for the best of wagers. It's a magnificent gamble. But, once I have placed my stakes on the
coming victory, what concern should I feel to find significance in the present? Merely to wager on the future does
not offer to old age or any period of life a strong, dynamic
view of life's responsibilities.

From time to time in the history of religion, sects have
appeared which openly reject all earthly responsibilities in
view of the glorious future. History recalls the harm and
confusion that this philosophy caused. You could join a
sect, or, which is much more likely in this period of religious indifferentism, you could go to the other extreme:
content yourself with an absolute minimum of observances.

But my interpretation of old age does not rest upon a
gamble, however noble. It views old age rather as a time of
life which exemplifies in countless ways a great principle
of our existence: *the principle of growth-through-diminishment.*

People, especially soil-tilling people, have always understood this principle, though they express it in varying ways.
No plant, no crop grows upon the farm unless something
has perished in order to give it life. According to an agri-
cultural genius of our age, the Swiss Dr. Ehrenfried Pfeiffer,
the central point in good farming is the compost heap. Out
of decayed vegetation comes the precious, new, fruitful
growth that enriches the farmer's barns. In turn, when this
growth is consumed by milk and beef cattle, it provides the
nourishing food for our table. Once more destroyed, and
organically digested, this transmuted nourishment appears
as the very fabric of our material organism.

[28]

Growth-Through-Diminishment

A certain decay or death is needed for the seed to come in contact with the life-giving forces, the various acids and alkalis in the soil. Growth-through-diminishment, factually, is a law of nature's organic system of existence as we know it. But the *meaning* of the law is derived from the new life that is released by the decay, the new life that is the principle of growth.

If this principle is applied to the evolution of plant and animal species, it is illustrated in myriad forms. The rocks record the disappearance of countless species which in turn leave room for newer and higher forms. The fact is obvious. The urgent question is: what is the principle that brings new life in place of the old?

Great scholars, like the late Fr. Teilhard de Chardin, have speculated on this point. I leave to others judgment to decide whether or not the scholars have found an adequate, wholly intelligible answer.

Is it unreasonable, then, to apply to old age the principle of strength-through-weakness? If the progress and magnificence of the world as we know it—the evolving and evolved world—have come into existence according to this principle, is it too much, then, for the humble and observant mind to apply a similar principle to the particular weaknesses, the particular defeats and diminishments of old age? Is it unreasonable to ask whether this lessening—in a certain way—of the individual human being, is not simply a prelude to, a prerequisite for, a new life of vastly increased power and existence?

In various picturesque forms, stories, parable, images, the Saviour recurs to this theme. The seed is buried in the ground; it dies there and decays, yet a new plant will arise from the seed's death. The teachings of the Son of Man will be rejected, His followers will be humiliated and killed, yet the sacred truths will triumph. The individual, if he loses his life, will find it. To him who gives, it will be given.

The seed is a victim of the soil; moisture and various chemicals attack and destroy the protective structure that houses the seed's inner kernel. But the very forces which destroy the seed's outer structure liberate its inner kernel, which is now free to sprout into the great world of light and air, and become a sun-drenched plant, or a wind-tossed giant of the forest. The seed that "fell where the soil was good . . . sprouted and grew," says Jesus (Mark 4:8), talking of the laws of growth for the Kingdom; and of His own death and resurrection (John 12:24): "Believe me, when I tell you this; a grain of wheat must fall into the ground and die, or else it remains nothing more than a grain of wheat; but if it dies, then it yields rich fruit." It is not the grain's kernel that has been conquered in the struggle with the earthy elements, the part that carries the inner force of indestructible vitality. That which has perished by the rude yet subtle forces of nature has liberated the true and vital kernel that neither wind nor storm nor erosion can nullify.

Growth-through-diminishment is the law of the Kingdom. But it has already been a principle in the history of God's dealings with the human race. The least people — least in power, in riches, in natural advantages — were chosen by the Creator to fulfill His designs through the centuries. The sterile wife, rejected and mocked by her more fortunate sisters, was honored by childbirth, even in her old age, by the birth of a prophet and master in Israel. The humble shepherd boy, not one of his boastful brethren, was chosen for kingship. The poor are trodden upon by the chariots of the mighty, yet they triumph where nothing remains of the mighty but a fading record. And so on; the Scriptures are full of this idea.

The laws of the Kingdom transcend merely human and natural laws. They surpass them, they move on heights that in no way are commensurate with earthly standards. As the Second Isaiah says: "For my thoughts are not your thoughts, neither are your ways my ways, says the Lord, for as the heavens are higher than the earth, so are my ways higher than your ways and my thoughts than your thoughts" (Isaiah 55:8, 9).

Yet the Kingdom's laws are in harmony with the great archetypal laws of nature. They surpass what is merely human, but they do not contradict it. In other words, if you want to understand and appreciate the laws of the Kingdom, you will do best if you familiarize yourself with the laws that govern humanity itself and the entire world of nature and its organic growth. If you know how the world of nature operates, if you have some perspective of human history in general, you will be in a better position to understand the operation of the spiritual Kingdom. The Saviour took His examples from the natural culture — physical, social, economic — around Him; He used, as did the great spiritual teachers of Israel, familiar phenomena of the forest, the sea, the fishing boat, the workbench, the merchant's store, the council chamber, the festival, and the funeral.

The most far-reaching utterances of the prophets and poets of the Bible attain their sublimity precisely because they are already rooted in knowledge of the way earthly things, human and non-human alike, are planted, grow, are seeded, multiply, and decay.

If old age nourished itself solely upon the leftovers of the feast of younger and more vigorous life, it would still have plenty to boast of, as is witnessed by the *De Senectute's* of all time. There are distinct and precious satisfactions in age that are peculiar to that period. Delights of memory are often keen: delights in old photographs, meeting with old friends, as well as the discovery of newer and deeper interpretations of matters which have long puzzled you. So the question I ask is by no means a derogation of what is, or at least can be for the more favored one, a real peace and happiness in later days. Nonetheless, the question as to what it all means still remains. The light of the dying embers has little comfort, if there is no new fire to be kindled. To understand the force of growth-through-diminishment, it is not enough merely to cite it as some kind of a magic formula. As such it would be interesting, but nonetheless meaningless, for it would remain as something merely magical or paradoxical. And it is also meaningless to deny the diminishment, and call it simply an illusion. The strength, the vitality of this principle is not derived from its apparent contradictions — for contradictions as such generate nothing but confusion. Growth-through-diminishment is alive, because it presupposes a living force, a life-giving, germinal force, which is the cause of the growth beneath and beyond the diminishment. The seed grows under the earth, because in the moisture and darkness it meets with life-giving forces. The seed assimilates these forces, incorporates them, uses them as building materials for a new structure that will sprout above the ground. New civilizations germinate from decaying cultures, not because decay as such contains the germs of the future, but because cultural or political decay has released new cultural or political forces hitherto unsuspected. The ancient Roman colonies had to fall to pieces, in ruins, in order that the new culture of Britain and Ireland should see the light. The death of old hopes allows new hopes to arise. Israel and Judah were crushed over and over again when they placed their confidences, as did their pagan neighbors, in merely human means, in horses and chariots and the keenness of weapons and the strength of warriors. But Israel and Judah rose again, whenever in the days of their "diminishment" they recalled the promises of God, bearing in mind that He had sworn to protect them, that He would be ever faithful, if they would but be faithful to Him.

In short, the power of this archetypal principle of growth-through-diminishment does not arise from some mysterious or mystical excellence which would attach to "diminishment" as such, for what is negative in its nature remains merely negative. Its power relies upon something altogether different; it rests upon the sworn word of the all-powerful Creator, who has given us a hope, a firm and unshaken hope. The strength of old age lies in the firmness of that hope; we cannot understand the meaning of age unless we explore the meaning of the hope itself.

[33]

Part II

OUR STEADFAST HOPE

The principle of strength-through-weakness is not a mere paradox, a formula invented to shock people out of their complacency. The truth, in our present existence, is never quite comfortable. Zen Buddhists use assertions flatly contradicting everyday experience as a means to arouse lazy minds to stimulating contemplation. Great religious teachers of all times had no hesitation at putting major truths in a paradoxical form, and our Saviour was no exception. "He who loseth his life shall find it," etc. The idea of a growth-through-diminishment, however, is based not upon a paradox but upon the affirmation of a positive, living force in the structure of the world. Its warrant for valid truth is the unshaken and unshakable faithfulness of the Creator toward His creatures; His fidelity to His own sworn promises.

The Bible has had more influence in human affairs than any other work ever written, if we speak of this collection of many books as a "work." Through all the rich variety of its many volumes, one unchanging note recurs: the fidelity of the Creator to the promises He made to His own people. "The Lord has sworn and will not repent." National and cosmic histories, personal narratives, moral treatises, lyrical and choral outbursts, parables, exhortations, prophecies,

[37]

love poems, tragedies — all emphasize in one way or another the tremendous drama of the Creator's unchanging fidelity to His own people, manifested by the eternal Master of Destiny.

Israel's entire tempestuous history was, and continues to be, based upon hope. As Christianity expanded, the implications of this hope extended to all who professed the Name and the faith of the Redeemer. The concept and content of this hope also increased immeasurably. But the principle remained the same: life, to be significant, and any epoch of life to carry meaning, will in some way reflect this supreme hope; will learn the precious hope bestowed upon it by the Creator's promises, by His very action in this world. The present moment can well be a time when we need to assert with special emphasis the validity of a life-philosophy based upon hope in the Biblical spirit precisely because of the pervasive influences, intellectual and cultural, that are brought to bear upon our life-philosophy, that deny or at least attempt to weaken our hope and as a substitute offer us despair.

In contrast to the notion that the prophet of despair is the true "realist," and hope is a sort of psychological affliction, one can well hold it important to emphasize, as do some of the great experts in the field of psychology and psychiatry, that the hopeful attitude to life — old age included — is the soundest even from the standpoint of psychology itself. A realistic view of sin, to look on it as a more or less deliberate moral choice that brings its own punishment, is by no means the same as the psychological disorder entitled a guilt complex. Sin from its very nature is a flat contradiction to hope. Yet the repented sin, the healed sin, is frequently the portal by which hope enters into our lives.

Karl M. Menninger, M.D., has noted that the Greeks for the most part considered hope an evil, and some of our latter-day poets shared "the fatalistic if not cynical view of the Greeks." Says the doctor: "I have had some patients who agreed with these poets. Partly that is why they were patients."

In the face of the cynics, the doctor affirms the therapeutic value of hope, and wisely distinguishes it, as I did above, from mere optimism. "The optimist, like the pessimist, emphasizes the importance of 'I.' But hope is humble, it is modest, it is self-less. Unconcerned with ambiguity of past experience, hope implies process; it is an adventure, a going forward, a confident search." Of his own state of Kansas, whose mental patient population has steadily decreased in the last fifteen years, he remarks: "We consider the crucial element in the Kansas State Hospital program to have been the inculcation of hope. Not in the patients directly, but in the doctors and all those who help them, in the relatives of the patients, in the responsible officials, in the whole community, and *then* in the patients. It was not just optimism; it was not faith, it was not expectations. We had no *reason* to expect what happened, and what still happens, and our faith was only that which all scientists share. But we did have hope."[1]

[1] Academic Lecture on "Hope" at the 115th annual meeting of the American Psychiatric Association, Philadelphia, Pennsylvania, April 7–May 1, 1959.

The doctor's words apply not ineptly to the entire condition of our aged population. It is not just a question of hope — in this case, a divinely inspired and grounded hope — in the persons of the aged themselves. It would mean hope *for* the aged, as well as a web of confidence that would envelope them, and affect not only their own personal attitudes, but the attitude of their families, their friends, of civil society, of the whole fabric of the world in which the aged live and move and have their being. Aging in a world of hope is a totally different affair from growing old in a world, in a community, in a network of family relationships poisoned by the bitter and unnatural atmosphere of despair.

The symbol of hope, the anchor, is the emblem of my native state of Rhode Island. I am not ashamed to see my whole attitude to present life-phases deeply influenced, indeed transformed, by the existence of a hope. This is not said to refer merely to a cheerful mood, a natural optimism. Such a mood has its advantages, but also its reverses and disappointments. I am speaking of hope in a full and integral sense; an expectation based on the knowledge of an assured certainty. People in Fidel Castro's Cuban prison were fortunate when they resisted the very urgent and natural inclination to despair. They "hoped," optimistically trusted that sometime, somewhere, they might be able to escape and find their way out to freedom. This mood was not a bad thing, it helped to sustain them, and keep them from demoralization. But it was very different from an objective hope experienced when by good fortune their ransom was paid, and they found themselves with a visa and an airplane ticket in their hands, ready to embark upon the coveted voyage. The visa and the ticket are still but "witnesses" — lowly objects that bear testimony to the reality of the future departure. But the hope they inspired was based on objective reality, and the subjective certainty that the ticket and the visa called forth was of a totally different category from that caused by a merely happy disposition.

My hope of the Resurrection — for myself and for all men who will avail themselves of it — lies in what the Redeemer has already done in the world's history, and what He, by His gift to me here and now of eternal life, has done for me.

There were skeptics in the first days of Christianity, who tried to soften or diminish or allegorize the message, just as there are today. But the declaration remains unchanged.

The Founder of Christianity made clear that you could not separate His teaching on the hope of future Resurrection from the rest of His life or message.

He demanded faith, belief — absolutely and unconditionally — that after death, as a certainty, we would each of us rise to an entirely new life; each of us as individual persons, yet enjoying the unity and peace of the future Kingdom. And if we have a hope based upon the solid foundation of that faith, we shall be grateful for each new day added to our lives.

The great St. Patrick, it is said, accepted both gain and loss in life with equal gratitude, because of his unshaken hope in the promises of God, Who had never deserted him. No matter how bitter the discouragement, Patrick knew that God's fidelity would never desert him, nor desert the people committed to his care. And he surprised the literal-minded and skeptical by his adherence to this principle.

The story is told of a wealthy pagan chieftain who thought he would try out the holy bishop's consistency on this point. So he sent Patrick a beautiful golden bowl all chased and carved with ancient Celtic, intricate, decorative designs. The saint unwrapped the package, and, when he saw the bowl, smiled benignly and said *"Grazagham!"* This word, I understand, was a contraction for the Latin expression *Gratias agamus Deo!* that is to say, Let us thank God!

When the servant returned, having journeyed over hill and dale, his master immediately questioned him. "And tell me now, what did the holy bishop say to you when you gave him the lovely bowl?" *"Grazagham* was all His Excellency said," replied the servant. "And nothing more?" queried the master. "Heaven knows that was all he said, just *Grazagham,"* replied the servant. "Then hitch the chariot up at once," cried the master, "and go, take the bowl back from him. If *that's* all the esteem he has for my beautiful gift!" So back hurried the servant to demand the bowl. Patrick again said *Grazagham* and immediately handed the precious present back to the servant without a further word. "And what did the holy bishop say *this time,* when you took the bowl away from him?" asked the master on his servant's return. "All he said was *Grazagham,"* replied the servant. The master stroked his curly beard for a while, and then exclaimed: "It's *Grazagham* when we give him the bowl and it's *Grazagham* when we take it away! That man is a saint of God. Drive me over to him at once so he can baptize me!"

So I accept each day as a gift, all my days as a gift, regardless of whether or not they bring me golden bowls. Each day is an opportunity to renew my confidence in the sworn word, the steadfast promises of the Creator. My attitude is not one of querulous questioning as to why I have not more days. But rather complete thanks that I have even another day in which to praise God, to love Him, to serve Him and fulfill His holy will. By the same token, I accept the temporary, limited burden of sorrow, humiliation, and the degree of punishment that accompanies my hope. These humiliating aspects of my human existence, these diminishments of old age, are so bound up with my future hopes that Paradise would be meaningless for me were it not in some way associated with this life's deprivations. Time, each day, each hour, is a gift, because it is in time, and through time's day-to-day vicissitudes, that the Creator works in us and for us the glory of the future life. The union of the two, the lofty destiny and the humble reality, is the mystery of the Creator's dealings with mankind. The union of the two elements — the promise of the transcendent future and the humiliations of our present condition — is not just a before-and-after affair. On the contrary, the great hope and the consciousness of our present state of humility are involved in all that we do and experience if we live according to our faith.

The affirmation of hope and the reality of present humiliations are intimately and dynamically associated. Great saints, the religious teachers of all times, in our Judeo-Christian tradition and in others as well, portray the approach to transcendent hope as made in and through the

[43]

portal of suffering and humiliation. It is *in* our littleness, that we encounter God. If we but cling firmly to this hope, we meet with Him in the darkest hours of life's pilgrimage.

A humble and observant mind, which is willing to look at life's changes quietly and steadily, will not yield to first impressions as to the negative character of old age. Is it unreasonable to expect such an observant mood? The mode, the apparatus of reasoning is different from that of the physical scientist, but the basic mood of observation need not differ, and the operation of our minds is largely determined by our moods. After all, it's the attitude you rightly expect in the scientist, an attitude of wonder, of anticipation, of expectant attention. Some of the greatest discoveries of our age were obtained by sudden mental revelation. In the collective advancement of human knowledge, imagination plays its part as does insight. But the bulk of the astounding scientific and technological superstructure that bewitches us in these days is the outcome of prolonged, patient observation, of ceaseless trial and verification.

The person of faith, too, is humble and observant, which would seem to be a reason why women — thoughtful and informed women — are often more successful than men in reaching the ultimate conclusions about life and death. A proud, impatient mind has little time for the idea of strength-through-weakness. But the Bible story through the centuries is woven about that theme. The least people — least among their powerful, boastful, political neighbors — all of whom have passed away leaving nothing but tombs and inscription — these humble folk have survived, and still bear witness to the Creator who spoke out of the burning bush and the shining clouds and the pillar of smoke to their ancestors.

The hope of the Resurrection — like the idea of growth-through-diminishment — is not foreign to that book that so steadfastly asserts the fidelity of the Creator's promises. On the contrary, the objective hope of the Resurrection was not unknown to the Jewish people from early times. When the Christian message was first announced by Jesus and His disciples, the idea of the Resurrection was by no means foreign to the Jewish people; that hope was an earnestly defended doctrine of the theological school of the Pharisees, in contrast to the resurrection-denying Sadducees. When Jesus announced that He Himself would rise again, and promised a share in the Resurrection to all who would accept His teaching and follow His example, He did not speak in mystifying terms. There was no uncertainty or dilution in the preaching of those chosen witnesses who proclaimed this divine promise for all His followers. It was not a cryptic or esoteric utterance.

The Saviour made plain that it was in our power, *now*, to accept or reject the glory of our future existence, which He had won for us by His life, His sufferings, and His cruel death. The glory of that future Kingdom was not something unrelated to this life. Rather the future glory of the Resurrection begins in this life, as a hidden seed planted in the ground, as a spring of living water raised from a deep well. This inner, present vitality, He taught, is connected with the future glory not in just some nominal or conventional fashion, like a ticket of admission to a play or dance. It is organically *one with it*. The *new life* begins now, right here in the midst of this changing and transient world.

Part III

THE POWER OF LOVE

"Love is the great fact in the world today," remarked the doctor, as we sat and talked on a windy December afternoon. "Love pours in from every side. It seems to me that we are enveloped in a great web or world of love. You meet love in places where you least expect it."

I knew the doctor well enough to be pretty sure she talked from conviction, not from mere sentiment. Moreover, when a doctor is also a patient in a city hospital women's ward, just recovering from having a leg amputated, with diabetes right around the corner, she is apt to be sober in her utterances. The doctor's two visiting friends and countrymen, a taxi driver and his wife, had, like her, left British Guiana almost a half century ago to try their luck in the States. They, too, paid the same tribute to love, as did a couple of other visitors who joined in the conversation. Framed distantly in the large hospital window that looked out over the swirling waters of New York's East River was the glass palace that houses the United Nations. How much of the great stream of love had poured in that building, through its various agencies; how much was vainly battering at its doors? Neither the convalescing doctor nor myself had the answer to that riddle.

[49]

Reflections on Growing Old

The United Nations, from its very nature, can be an instrument of selfishness, a theater of political scheming. Those political specialists who met in San Francisco and founded this ever-increasing organization clearly saw such a possibility. They erected such safeguards as they found feasible against the perversion of a work of peace to an instrument of dissension. Some UN safeguards against selfishness have been successful, others have failed. Nonetheless, the present United Nations stands as a monument to a conviction that a certain degree of love — not the highest, not sufficient for the strenuous struggle of principle with power-seeking and ambition, yet nonetheless a certain degree of love — can win out, and will win out, in spite of all the handicaps stacked against it.

As I reflected on that conversation, it seemed to me that certain assertions can and should be made concerning love of neighbor in its relation to old age. The thoughts came naturally enough. One might sum them up in several propositions.

1. Old age has at its disposal the exercises of the *greatest social power* in the world, that of genuine love for one's fellow human being. This love is inspired by the Creator's own love for us, and His willingness to become one of us and share our joys, our experience, and our suffering.

2. Love is powerful, as a world force, only when it is understood in its *full dimensions:* its depth, breadth, and length as well as its sublime height. It loses out when twisted or counterfeited. Its dimensions cover the entire complexity of our existence: our nature and rights quite as well as our more purely individual relationships.

3. This world force *operates in the world today*, far more, as the doctor herself remarked, than we suspect; yet far less than would be the case if it were better known, if the concept were not minimized and distorted.

4. Love's world-power springs not just from our inner resources, but also from without: from its being the *presence of eternal life*. When we truly love our neighbor, the Eternal Himself enters our lives — "there am I in the midst of you" — and lifts us to a share in His own life, the life of the future Resurrection.

1. LOVE AS A GIFT

Much can be said about love as a great and holy gift. Spiritual books describe the visit of St. Anthony of the Desert, at the age of 95, to his desert companion, St. Paul, the first Christian hermit, aged 100, and the meal they took together. They were duly refreshed by an entire loaf that the raven brought as they conversed at the spring, instead of the daily half loaf the raven had habitually rationed out to Paul in his solitude. The never-failing gift of bread was a sign of the Father's love for those who abandon all earthly goods in order that they may possess Him, and Him alone. Very many centuries later another contemplative hermit, the formerly dissipated French officer, Charles de Foucauld, also meditated in the African desert and conceived a new way to bring that same message of love direct into the heart of the humanly most inaccessible regions of the modern world. In old age, as in these contemplations of the desert, you learn, as Charles de Foucauld said, "to see things as they are." You learn how varied, how real is that most precious of possessions, the divine gift of love for your neighbor.

Since these are rather apocalyptic days — people phone me and ask if the end of the world is not coming — it is well for us all, young and old, to remember that the matter upon which we shall be questioned at the Last Judgment is precisely the degree to which we have, or have not, tangibly shown the love of neighbor. "Did you visit Me when I was destitute, when I was sick, when I was in prison . . . ?"

If you yourself are elderly, you will naturally think first and foremost about the kind of love that is rationed out to the aged themselves. Love, that is to say, on the recipient side. Some may argue that not so much love is needed in these times: look at what is provided for the aged that they did not enjoy in earlier and less comfortable periods. Yes, in a sense this is true. In our times, the aged benefit by all sorts of pleasant or useful conveniences, especially in quarters that are planned expressly for them. They don't have to climb stairs, awkward step-downs are avoided. In prosperous times and communities, they enjoy modern lighting and communication facilities. Nourishment suited to advanced years is more easily obtained. Means are at hand for useful occupations, recreations, travel, that we little knew a couple of generations ago. As for medical and hospital care, there is no comparison in the variety and ingenuity of relief that is provided, and the ease with which it is obtained; that is to say, when you *are* in a position to enjoy these benefits. The rationality and variety of these provisions for old age's comfort throw into the harshest possible light the plight in our times of the great percentage of the aged who do not enjoy them, even in our own generally prosperous country and, to a much greater extent, throughout the world.

Age strips you of certain joys and privileges. But of the greatest privilege, age, as a rule, cannot wholly rob you. Advanced years give an extra opportunity to make the love of neighbor your own, in new and unexpected ways, and one way is the relief of loneliness for other aged persons. Modern means of communication have, indeed, done much to decrease the terrors of loneliness, but they have not entirely abolished it. Few are the aged who do not suffer from solitude in some degree. The longer you live, the more of your old friends and acquaintances drop off. The more frequently do you pick up the paper and read the death notices of folk considerably younger than yourself. Or you just drift apart.

Yet you can do much to mitigate the bitter loneliness of old age; you can at least ease its frightening, absolute character. Such simple means of communication are available as a casual note or letter, a short visit, remembrance of an anniversary; or, from time to time, a longer conversation, where again you can check over the past. Or the telephone call.

In old age, the telephone can play a larger part in your personal life than it did in your younger and more agile years. If you avoid the danger of piling up service expenses (and how rapidly they mount!) you can communicate in a comfortable manner with old friends, and even with mere acquaintances, in a way you could not enjoy if you were dependent upon only face-to-face conversation. You can congratulate friends on their birthdays, inquire for their health, at least make them feel you are still interested in them. With patience and knowledge, you can answer a considerable number of inquiries, out of whatever store of knowledge may still cling to your elderly mind. Not that the quality of conversation has necessarily improved since the days of the Athenian Academy or the all-night colloquy of St. Scholastica with her saintly brother, Benedict, while the rain fell in torrents outside the monastery walls. The timbre of conversation, like the ring of true charity, is an absolute, not dependent on epochs for tuning. But *occasions* for conversation and its implications for human living expand rapidly in our days. Unless we meet this expanded opportunity, we may be false to the integrity of charity itself.

As I write these words, a friend mentions to me that for a month or so before a mutual friend's death, after a lingering illness, "each morning she so appreciated my telephoning her — just a reminder, but a reminder in a great solitude. . . ." Incidentally, I learned from another source that our mutual friend asked, as a special favor, that she might be taken from her private room to the women's ward of the hospital, so, as she said, "she could die in good company."

Society, for better or worse, has developed a sort of ritual for recalling periodically common memories: Christmas, birthdays, various anniversaries, and jubilees. But these events are just a symbol of all that can be evoked in the panorama of human communication, as the various peoples of the world become more and more present to one another. It would seem inevitable that in the future, intercommunicating world, the older generations will play an important part, and play it even while their ability for any kind of strenuous action has waned.

As you advance in years, you are apt to be impressed by the great number of older women who live alone or virtually alone in our vibrant contemporary world. Some, it is true, have built up personal associations — family, cultural, professional — with the years. These associations stand them in good stead at the decline in their lives. For some, solitude comes suddenly, through widowhood or some other form of deprivation. Or they just drift into their lonely existence, and find themselves really isolated. Yet no human being can stand continual isolation without distress. Hell may be "other people," *les autres,* in the words of Sartre, but "hell" can even more be one's own total loneliness.

Responsibility toward aged women deserves special emphasis, since, after all, it is easily met, with a little planning and forethought. How much can be accomplished by an occasional visit, an opportunity to talk of old acquaintances, a bit of the hundred-and-one ways by which a spark of sunshine may be brought into desolate lives! So much comfort comes from feeling yourself as somehow a member of a group, however small and apparently unimportant: so much can be obtained for so little.

[55]

Yet we are not fair to this topic if we pass over what older and isolated people can do to help their own situation. Even though what one can give to others appears small, it can be great in the sight of God.

The woman who in her younger years has cultivated some positive interest in helping her fellow human beings will suffer far less from loneliness than one whose life has been concentrated upon herself and her own immediate friends and relatives.

The ever-growing industrialization and specialization of society tend to isolate the aged, if they allow themselves to be isolated. On the other hand, the same "complexification," with its vastly increased opportunities for intercommunication — by word, by writing, even by travel — offers to nearly every woman of good will *some* opportunity for reaching and helping some other isolated person, in the ocean of human suffering and misery. There is practically always someone, somewhere, whom you can befriend; if you do not know of anyone, agencies and organizations can inform you.

Not only do such interests draw us out of ourselves, they place us in relation to other people. I am not urging elders to join committees, but rather suggesting that *some* form of interpersonal contact with those in need — materially or spiritually — can mean so much not only for those whom you befriend, but for yourselves as well. So often an older woman can, with little risk or effort, be a bridge between distant groups.

Hence the importance in one's younger years of forming

wide interests, so as not to be caught short when life around you seems to fade.

Much remains to be learned, by intelligent investigation, about the secrets — psychological, cultural, religious — that have enabled married couples to preserve their unity and mutual helpfulness into an advanced age, or rather, to grow in spiritual unity and mutual love. What is the secret of Nettie (aged 83) and Arthur (aged "almost 93"), both retired government clerks? Just as I write these lines I receive — in a clear, though a bit shaky, hand — their semi-annual greetings, "still counting our many blessings," though "Arthur has been over four years in his easy chair," and Nettie finds it none too good with her arthritis. A widow and a widower, they had joined forces in late life, and discovered a bliss which even yet seems unshaken. "How did God happen to make a woman so devoid of faults as Nettie?" mused Arthur one day when he was in his buoyant seventies, and Nettie reciprocated, though as a quondam country schoolteacher she had to admit that Arthur "does get a bit forgetful at times." I first met Nettie when, as a young Southern white farm widow, she taught, and taught most efficiently, in a primitive, one-room, Negro school. With the help of the bigger boys she stacked up the old school stove in chilly winter weather. I think she must have stacked up quite a supply of love in those hard early days, too, and Arthur now is the beneficiary.

Says the French physician, Dr. René Biot, if you ask such couples how have they achieved this harmonious result, they will answer very humbly, but very sincerely, that they have "not done anything notable or special." This is true in the sense that they haven't utilized this or that particular method, they haven't supplied this or that recipe. They have "simply" (I put the words in quotes so as to emphasize its full bearing) done day after day that which up to then was a common task, that is to say, they were devoted each to the other and both, in union, to their children. Hour after hour, they have carried out the work that was necessary for this end. Certainly, they encountered a succession of difficulties. Life is like that. But they did what lay within them to endure these setbacks with the maximum of courage and without any attempt to dramatize them. And when some happy occasion came along, they welcomed it humbly and peaceably, they enjoyed it together . . . "very simply," they would again say.

If, says Dr. Biot, you probe a little further as to the sources of this conjugal serenity, you find that the aged couple will confide to you — "with still more humanity and a more convincing conviction — that it was the grace of God working within them, and you will feel like kneeling down with them to thank the Lord for thus having consummated their 'unity.' "[1] I would not be tempted to quote, incidentally, this good French author if in the course of a long priestly life I had not often shared the same experience of happy old married couples, who despite all sorts of obstacles have made joy triumph over the inroads of time.

Mention of elderly couples naturally raises the question

[1] R. Biot, *La Vieillesse: Problème d'aujourd'hui*, Spes, Paris, 1961. p. 244.

whether or not it is to the best interest of all concerned that the older and the younger generations live together in the same household, or whether they are happiest when they dwell separately. There is so much discussion on this point, and such a variety of opinions. Evidently there are great advantages to be gained by separate households. Young couples who start out on their joint career, can plan together, and are not impeded by the presence under the same roof of the older generation. Immediate and daily conflicts of convenience and temperament are avoided. Older folk living by themselves can adjust so many matters for their own comfort. In many cases, the ideal seems to be separate living, but near enough to the younger people not to be isolated, to be available for frequent visiting.

On the other hand, comfortable arrangements make us lose sight of the other side of the picture. This is the immense benefit to both old and young of daily companionship, in accordance with a tradition that exemplifies certain ideals of the larger family. For the young, older people are a distinct refuge. You can go to them with certain personal problems that it is not quite fair to propose to the parents themselves. Elders can remember when your parents were themselves children, so that some of the strange things parents insist upon make more sense when approached from this somewhat unusual point of view. The elders were *themselves* once young, and Grandfather remembers that once he could balance an eel on the point of his nose.

If the different generations are to live happily together, older folk need to know the differences that do separate them from the young. For the young are distanced not merely by the natural circumstances of youth, but by an entirely different culture from that in which the elders grew up.

We may deplore this difference, but it is a plain fact, and is above and beyond the ordinary course of human history. Words have a different meaning for the younger generation, or at least different connotations. The young of today are separated from the elders by World War II, and the inconceivably rapid developments of the postwar period: cultural, political, ideological. For those of us who predate even World War I, this difference is all the more noticeable.

Today's youth live in, and are living in, a world and a set of cultural standards that we gave them. Because of today's rapid changes, we are charged with the duty, and the privilege, to keep these standards clear and uncontaminated: this is the great responsibility of the older generation, and it is a privilege as well.

The elders could then permit themselves, for instance, certain liberties which, in our time, did not bring the immediate and devastating consequences that such indulgence does today. A bit of excess drinking, for instance, has a very different meaning for youth at the controls of a speeding automobile than it had for youth in more leisurely times, when the good old carriage horse would bring the somewhat confused driver home. It was the older people, not the young, who created the demoralizing urban conditions that still "breed" juvenile delinquency. It was the older folk whose educational policies have affected our ideal of the American home. If we frankly recognize these mistakes and their effect upon the younger generation, there still remains the great and sacred task of passing on to them the best that we have.

The Second Vatican Council has emphasized for us a world of mutual help that over the years has been greatly neglected: that of friendly intercourse with people of other faiths, who share with us belief in God and some of our deepest religious and moral convictions. If more of that sharing had been done in the past, the world's religious forces would not be as they are today, a prey to their own misunderstandings. I am not speaking of honest differences, but of those human weaknesses that frank and friendly conversation can minimize, even if it cannot abolish.

For peace and happiness in those latter years let me remember that the phenomena that trouble me — the diminishments and burdens proper to old age — are not something that has just happened to me personally; they are the common lot of mankind, for better or worse, and thus form a meeting ground for all other human beings. Still more is it vital for me to understand that through the medium of this commonly shared human experience, interpreted and supported by a God-given and steadfast hope, I come into closer contact, if I so wish, with the development in men of a new life: the life of divinely given charity, the vitality of the Creator Himself imparted to His creatures! imparted, that is to say, as the life of the vine is imparted to its branches.

If we are fearful we can retreat to a less and less consciously active part in human affairs. What used to be accomplished by the free, generous impulse of charitable-hearted individuals is then taken over by a great network of civic institutions. These are run as agencies of the city or of the state, thus leaving a *relatively* smaller part for private and personal charity to play in human affairs. Love will then be less missed if it departs, leaving a fragrant memory. So we erect a touching monument to Crimea's Florence Nightingale and to New Orleans' Margaret Haugherty, and are happy that these jobs are now done scientifically, according to rules and forms we have derived from expert analysis of human conditions.

We could very well succeed in abolishing altogether the idea of personal love, as something foreign to the spirit of 1984—and what a catastrophe to the human spirit that would be!

2. THE DIMENSIONS OF LOVE

Even yet, the dimensions of love, so dramatically outlined by the Apostle Paul, are far from being adequately surveyed. The love that we as human beings extend to any form of human need or distress extends by the same token to all the phases of man's being: in groups, in communities, in society, in the world at large.

Types of misery prevail in our time which in point of fact are connected with great patterns of modern progress, such as the dislocation, crowding, and demoralization that belong to proletarian migration and in-migration. Unless we are complete pessimists, we hope and trust that time, thought, and good will can find a remedy for these disorders. Anyhow, political scheming and byplays aside, we proceed on this assumption.

Certain elements of human unhappiness, such as sin, death, and taxes, will always be with us, not to speak of racial and political antagonisms and the ever-lurking threat of war.

At the same time, science — political, physical, medical, etc. — continues steadily to check off the percentage of incurables, to enlarge the areas of human living where one can reasonably expect to be spared any great suffering.

Is this Utopia? No. Is it meaningless? Also no. Humanity has already paid an enormous debt of suffering and penance for its primal sins, and for the sins that followed thereafter. If we ever escape from the present nuclear nightmare, may not the time come — if not impeded by our own continuing perversity — when this burden of human debt will be lessened? And does not the Creator's love extend also to the good in man, as it extends to the good in the cosmos as a whole? There is a theological theory, with arguments to support it, that the world grows steadily worse and worse before the final transformation. But is this *necessarily* so, also from a theological standpoint? If certain conditions are fulfilled, if men do finally learn something of peace and wisdom, may not the ultimate preparation be also in relative peace? Is it necessary that the human race should be floundering in division and spiritual destitution when the Saviour arrives for the second coming? Will half the virgins at the time of His coming be still foolish, or will they have finally learned to save for themselves some of the oil of wisdom?

Some may object to the idea that I place so vast an area of social action, such as that for the indigent aged, under the broad scope of love. Yet the great St. Augustine himself, who was no social sentimentalist, did not hesitate to assign this immense role to the love of God, precisely because of his broad concept of its many dimensions. As he wrote (*On the Morals of the Catholic Church*, XV, 25):

"I hold virtue to be nothing more than a perfect love of God. For the fourfold divisions of virtue, I regard as taken from four forms of love. For these four virtues, I should have no hesitation in defining them: that temperance is love giving itself entirely to that which is loved; fortitude is love readily, proudly bearing all things for the sake of the love object; justice is love serving only the loved object, and therefore ruling rightly; prudence is love distinguishing with sagacity between what hinders it and what helps it. The object of this love is not anything but only God, the chief good, the highest wisdom, the perfect harmony. So we may express the definition thus: that temperance is love keeping itself entire and incorrupt for God; fortitude is love bearing everything readily for the sake of God, justice is love serving God only, and therefore ruling well all else, as subject to man; prudence is love making a right distinction between what helps it towards God and what might hinder it."

Indeed, says the same St. Augustine (*On the True Religion*, XLVI, 87):

The Power of Love

"The rule of love is that one should wish his friend to have all the good things he would wish to have himself, and should not wish the evils to befall his friend he wishes to avoid himself. No evil must be done to any. Love of one's neighbor worketh no evil (Romans 13:10)."

Much of any prophecy depends upon the courage and wisdom of mankind to see it fulfilled. It is easy to counterfeit love: easy to reject any form of love that disturbs our comfort in favor of mere pietism and unwillingness to soil one's hands with the dust and callouses of honest action. Easy, too, to invent substitutes; pseudo-charities, that take care of the material part of man and neglect his spiritual and religious nature, that practice basic inhumanity under the guise of a considerate humanism.

In this present, developing world, the dynamic power of divine love is as yet only imperfectly apprehended. Absolutely speaking, those who *do* know its power are numerous: they are scattered over the surface of the globe, they are found right in our own cities and communities, right in our local parishes. Absolutely they are impressively numerous. Their number is growing. And their power, the power of the growing seed, the power of the hidden Kingdom, the power of the Creator working silently in His own creation, is beyond our narrow ken.

"I came to cast fire upon the earth," said the Saviour, "and what better can I wish than that it be kindled?"

That fire is burning in countless pin points around the world, even though His great flame as yet is not kindled. It will not be extinguished by any amount of bitterness and violence. Indeed, its greatest enemy is not violence, but sheer listlessness and timidity. And there is so much that older people can do, precisely because of their "diminished" life, to spread the appreciation of real love of neighbor, to contribute to the magic spark by which it can burst into flame. After all, it was the aged and rheumatic brother porter Alfonso Rodriguez, who kindled, by his conversation during study years in Majorca, Pedro Claver to consecrate his life to the task of redeeming souls and bodies of Cartagena's shiploads of utterly miserable African slaves.

In this age especially, as in all preceding periods, the concept of love is not to be diminished or modified to suit the supposed spirit of the times. Nor is it to be forced into some sort of a narrow, truculent mold as an ideology or enthusiasm to be publicized as a world-saving discovery. I believe the time calls for something very different, yet very old. *In order that love may take its rightful place as a life-giving force, a creative force, we must now — as at other turning points in history, but now most especially — make every effort to see love in all its vast varied and world-embracing dimensions.* This is not a spectacular program, but one infinitely far-reaching.

If love is to keep its place in our world economy, love must realize its manifold dimensions and what they imply in the changing world in which we live. For the *full* meaning of love contains the ultimate key to the meaning of old age.

We are fortunate when the two great forces — of love, and of political and social responsibility — coincide and harmonize their efforts for the benefits of the aged, or any other needy element in our community. But we are not so fortunate when these respective forces conflict. Religious love would be very unhappy, for instance, if the civil government felt a duty, a "civil responsibility," to ease suffering old people quite out of this rough world (I believe the Shakespeare text variant is "tough" world) by providing them with gratis-operated mercy killings or euthanasia. (Do you pay for those pseudo-medical services in advance?) A pluralistic civil society would not be so happy if one or the other religious denomination were to utilize state alms facilities for the propagation of a particular sect. On the contrary, would believers be happy if the doctrinaire secularists were to succeed in depriving the aged in state-subsidized institutions from even the non-discriminating spiritual care which is their natural right?

These, you would say, are extreme cases. Still the possibility of such conflict between the forces of love and the dynamism of political and social structure is by no means a matter of mere imagination. A conflict can arise in the future as it has arisen in the recent past, through the eruption of various crazes and ideologies that sweep aside all carefully plotted boundaries between the respective forces.

The ways, the language, the folk customs, and the immensely varied institutions which express to the modern world the spirit of divinely inspired love have become so much a part of our civilization that I think we are apt to lose sight of its possible destruction, *as a force*, as a tangible force, in our public life. We need only look at the welfare projects of Soviet Russia or recall those of Nazi Germany to see what I mean. Mussolini's workers' program *Dopo Lavoro*, "After Working Hours," was in many ways splendidly conceived, the kind of thing that emerged quite naturally in a country like Italy that already had a long tradition of practical charity. Yet the program hung perilously on the border between good and evil. It could fulfill its best purpose, as a fine example of what civilization can do for its workers when it still keeps the forms and atmosphere of respect for the human person, or it could become charity's ugly counterfeit, public welfare skillfully utilized as an instrument of political ambition and domination.

Ignorance bears more of the blame than we are quite ready to acknowledge.

We are ignorant, unaware, for the most part, of the force that love can be in this world, a force like that of the ocean rising tide: advancing by gently lapping waves, not even noticeable as you watch it, yet steadily advancing and capable of lifting any burden that the ingenuity of human engineering can float upon it. Unaware, that is to say, of the infinite variety and subtlety of ways by which such love can and does cope with the most rooted and desperate problems of human living. Unaware of the lives of those great men and women who have accomplished "miracles" of love in the past, but most of all unaware of what is occurring at the present time.

The image of love can also be distorted from another angle. Without directly assailing the key idea of love in the name of social optimism, like the Communists, or of social

[68]

pessimism, like the Nazis; without any direct assault upon its integrity, the virtue, the divine gift of love can become so much a matter of the individual, of a person's purely internal life, as to lack any pertinence to the complicated world we live in. Just a beautiful dream, a poetic vision, as it were; not a live and conquering force in our civilization.

Is love then to be "spiritualized," made a sort of emanation of the other world, irrelevant to any earthly circumstances except possibly moments of great sorrow? Is it to be just a blessing on wedding anniversaries, or an ornament to college commencements? Or on the contrary is it to be forced into the mold of a social gospel, to be weighed and measured by the amount of temporary, tangible benefit it may succeed in engineering?

Confusion can be caused by ideas of love rigidly adapted to another age or culture, which have been passed down without proper modifications to later centuries. The charity of the Byzantine Empire, or of the monks of the Christian East, was noble and often sublime. Some of its features put our Western habits to shame, especially its deep sense of the fellowship created by membership in the Mystical Body of Christ. Yet methods for relieving hunger and poverty that would be suited to an early imperial economy are quite inadequate for the needs of our present interlocking and growing society, a society that apparently doesn't bat an eye at the proposal to spend $20 billion of the public money on the single project of putting a couple of men on the moon. Hence a too-narrow concept of love's scope can fall an easy prey to the reproaches of a modern efficiency expert.

Love, therefore, must be total — without loopholes or escapes — if it is to survive the dissolving influences of a rapidly expanding human and physical world. It must be total, if it is to meet the tremendous challenge of that world, and lead the world upward towards self-realization under God, and not contribute to disaster by its own defeat. The principle at issue is the complete vision of what love is *meant* to be, in our times, in our circumstances, rather than a detailed catalogue of all that is implied in the complete vision. For if we know what virtues and what action charity is *supposed* to include, by its very nature, a lifetime of experience is ahead to work out its implications. Relieving obvious distress is certainly one of the noblest works of love, of a type which, despite all social benefits, we shall always need to have with us. Yet it is equally noble, and often much more of the nature of true love, to do what one can to set peoples' minds straight on crucial ethical issues. It is a great and grand thing to supply food to working people thrown out of their jobs and suffering penury because of a prolonged strike or lockout. But the work of the expert or specialist who works unselfishly days and nights in order to find an equitable and practical solution to a vexed problem of conflicting rights and duties — such a consecrated work — supposing it is done in true equity and not in any selfish spirit — can be a work of the utmost love. The arbitrator's toil may not only avert misery from countless suffering families, it may also thwart the machinations of antisocial forces that profit by class conflicts: and it may inspire new hope, new trust, into the minds of a whole nation. Through the truly honest and un-selfish arbitrator's work the hand of God can be truly operating.

The idea I am expressing here can be easily distorted, and subtly made to say the opposite of what is meant to be expressed. An arbitration, a government, a business, a profession run by "love" rather than justice, is a negation of justice and can all too readily become a hateful tyranny. Where justice and rights are ignored, love is cruelly carica-tured. But if man is loved with his full panoply of rights and duties, where justice, not mere sentiment, dictates, love is exercised in its genuine breadth and depth. The school superintendent, the corporation lawyer, the actor, the drill operator in a factory, who do their honest work for God, are true lovers of mankind.

If we truly love people — children, grown-ups, aged — we must love them in their entirety. We must love them in their whole being, their institutions, as far as these are just; their legal wisdom, their culture: all that is truly human and the result of man's triumph over barbarism. We must love those traditions that people have inherited from the past, from Greece or Rome or Judea or from the wisdom of other continents and other lands, not omitting the wis-dom of our own native America. The prophet Samuel scolded the people of Israel when they became impatient with the rule of their own judges, and were infatuated with the idea of enthroning a king in imitation of their pagan neighbors. Samuel told them in unvarnished lan-guage the kind of servicing the proposed king would exact from them: young and old, men and women. Nevertheless, he directed them to respect the king once they had chosen one, and helped them in the selection. King Saul wasn't such a happy choice, after all; but then they had asked for it.

The comprehensiveness, the dimensions of true love, are much like the air we breathe. Love is available to us as agents, not merely as beneficiaries, in all phases and circumstances of our lives; and, in its own distinctive fashion, in old age, again in active form, not merely on the receiving end.

Old folk can immeasurably aid the cause of peace if they will but set the example. Long experience, and the endurance of rebuffs in their own case, can make them more ready to understand what other people suffer who because of their race, creed, or nationality are rebuffed in the ordinary contacts of life. As they draw near to the fountain of eternal life, they can be more ready to understand and sympathize with people who for unreasonable causes are deprived, through ignorance or malice, of even an approach to that fountain.

If love is shoved aside, then, as a thing of no moment, it is because we have conceived it on too small and restrictive a scale, or because it has been caricatured. Love is not exclusively a business of repairing human wreckage, physical or moral, but of enabling people to withstand temptation, to build homes and families, to live as human beings under the conditions that the Creator has destined for them here on earth.

If our concept of love is narrow, if its scope is restricted to a few individual and conventional acts of kindness, or if it takes refuge in purely internal piety, it will be powerless before the immense challenge flung at it, before the complexity of the modern world's interrelated problems. It will be equally powerless if it takes refuge and evaporates in emotional myths. Its power consists in being itself, in reaching its full scope of infinite patience; in ascertaining the factual truth; in planning singly and jointly for dealing with the situation in question; in acting boldly, unselfishly, and with infinite patience both with one's own personal limitations and with the limitation of others with whom one plans and co-operates. Love deals not with abstractions, but with living minds and hearts of fellow human beings, and these can only be learned by going out of ourselves, as it were, and entering into the situation and problems of people who are often of totally different background. Even so simple an expression as the word "bread" for instance, has a vastly different meaning to the well-fed guest at the lunch-counter here at home, for whom bread is merely a slight appendage to a meal for better handling of your food, and bread for starving millions who would consider themselves fortunate if they could secure even a handful of rice. If you returned from Europe right after World War II you may remember the curious pang that seized you when you saw whole slices of bread tossed into our city garbage pails.

Love is not only important, it is necessary. Its absence is a total loss. I could feel happy if anything I said or wrote, as a priest or as a citizen, would arouse people to even one greater degree of charity — to more frequent, to more ingenious manifestations; if I could inspire them to take at least one old person under their personal charge. Again, if I could inspire the older folks to be charitable one to the other; to live in humble peace, and not in bitter criticisms, mutual gossip.

Many human elements beside love make up the world we live in, and help to make latter years tolerable. All the conveniences of civilization contribute to the comfort of my present life: food, clothing, transportation, medical service, postal facilities, books and libraries, legal protection, governmental administration, civil security. *Per se* these are not gifts of charity; they are my right, my natural heritage as a citizen, as a member of a civilized community. In similar fashion, I could list the benefits that accrue to me as a member of my religious community, the Church.

Yet an old age without love is a mockery. The bitter irony is that so many uncounted millions of old people in the world must experience just that absence of love; even if they succeed in useful or at least intelligent employment, the society in which they live is merging into barbarism.

We may differ as to the point whether aid should come from the younger members of the family or from the local community, from the church organization, from the state or the national government. But aid and comfort for the aged in some shape or form is an elemental human necessity, just as are institutions for the young, employment for adults, or care for the sick and disabled.

Charity — the love of God and man — is not something peculiar to the last stage of our existence. But in our latter years we have the opportunity, and the privilege, to explore new corners of its immense dimensions. I am inclined to agree with the opinion set forth by a number of distinguished theologian-psychologists that the life of charity is not dependent upon our psychic condition. Even the obstacles created by our declining forces create the occasion for the development of new phases of one's spiritual life.

The learned French Dominican, Fr. Corvez, is very positive on the presence of these new occasions. It belongs to the very essence of charity, he says, to its inmost structure and dynamism, to continue to grow without ceasing. And charity grows all the more rapidly as it approaches the terminus of its movement. God draws the soul all the more powerfully as the soul "approaches nearer to him by the dimensions of its charity." There are no limits to the grace of God nor to the power of the soul to receive it. The deprivations of age, says the same author, do not prevent our persevering interest in the great ideal forces that operate in the world and drive the world forward towards its destiny. With spiritual maturity we find a more attractive and easier way to go to God, free from the depressing weights and the delays of our first steps upward. "Grace pushes toward its term," says Corvez, and one feels a "passionate interest for the real values of life." You'll be a lot more selective in reading the news columns. But you will be much more conscious as to what's cooking behind the scenes.

Spiritual maturity is not an automatic process. Though stoutly armed, Albrecht Dürer's aged knight rides through a wilderness of possible deceptions, psychically regressive monsters who will be only too happy to drag him from his horse and trample him underfoot. Each of us, as he approaches this final term, must battle with his own particular form of selfishness, the habits that one has allowed to accumulate through the years, those elements which of their nature tend to decrepitude and to spiritual death. Yet these inner monsters can be known and can be resisted. Humility and simplicity, not elaborate ingenuity, best fit us for the winnowing and keep us from making vain excuses.

3. LOVE OPERATES IN THE WORLD

Some of you may have watched a TV documentary film shown over national networks early in December, 1962. Entitled "The Superfluous Ones," it brought the viewer face to face with individuals, young and old, who, in one way or another, represented the various types of people for whom the metropolis spells loneliness, aimlessness, or neglect. The elderly housewife, displaced by urban-renewal upheavals, bitterly mourned the loss of her lifelong, beloved neighborhood. Aimless, spiritless youths spelt out in their own lives the wretched consequences of dropping out from school beforetime. These, and many others, were the "superfluous ones": the people we forget, the people for whom no ready answer or institutional care is at hand. But, in a curious paradox, the utterly unconcerned, normal, happy, loving and lovable orphans in their cribs were the "superfluous" ones in a gravely deeper sense. For the vista of their future lacked the least spark of earthly hope, save for the privileged few who might find a home. Only a few years would roll by until these squirming, shouting little ones would be thrown out on their own, in a demoralizing world that had closed its doors against them before they could even peek inside. They were the first to appear on the screen, and they were the last, and as yet for the majority of them no wise worker had come forth with a satisfactory solution.

You don't need to embark on a slumming expedition to discover, from where I live, these and other types of the "superfluous ones." A ten-minute walk or a short bus ride can bring for you similar confrontations.

I am not putting it up to the aged to cope with these staggering problems; so many of the older folk have enough problems of their own. Nevertheless, as I watched the pictures unroll, I could not help thinking that these troubled figures had a word to say to the elders as well. For normally all can heighten our gift of understanding. It is only in the later years that you can fully appreciate how deeply disturbing it must be to find all your old associations rudely severed, to have your lot cast with people who, for all your intents and purposes, are complete strangers, and to have to try in some manner to reconstruct your life from the ground up. By the same token you learn there is so much that the aged can do to relieve human misery. True, they may feel themselves, and may really be, on the rim of things, yet the quality of their charity may make up for its enfeebled quantity.

If the world-transforming powers of divine charity are such a force, comparable to nothing else on earth, why do *good* people, if I can call them such, so often fail to let it operate? More precisely, if it is accessible to all of us at all times of life, even to the very end, why do we neglect that source of spiritual power? How can we deprive ourselves and the rest of mankind of such a privilege? I put the question in that way, because I consider it most important; because I think we ought not to pass the matter rapidly by with some casual explanation, but ought to pause awhile and ask ourselves where the trouble lies. For an old age that receives no charity is obviously unhappy, like the characters we saw in "The Superfluous Ones." But even more unhappy is the unspeakably tragic old age that knows no practice of love, even in the mitigated or diminished form that old age necessarily imposes. A wealthy Catholic man who died intestate a few years ago in New York City, leaving an estate of $32 million, was a type of "superfluous one" more miserable, in fact, than any dispossessed wanderer. But without reaching such a state of utter futility, so many aged — not innately selfish, not of bad will, perhaps full of a certain quota of kindly velleities — pass into the world beyond without having made use of the opportunities that lie at hand.

I am not talking of formal "charities," the responses that you may or may not make to the tide of Christmas or Easter appeals that float gently upon your desk, most of them on their way to the wastebasket. But I mean those personal actions and contacts — or words or deeds — developments in the new and endlessly complexified world. Our concepts of what is meant by charity are so restrained, so conventional, so limited by conventions derived from the past; and, by that token, expositing our immense treasure to contempt or ridicule. If we love our young people, for instance, we shall love them not just affectionately grouped around the family fireside — or what takes the place of one in our modern world-flitting civilization — but love them in the full development of their personalities, their future careers, their own perspectives of the future: in their inner battles and conquests or failures.

As God's love for man has no limit in its intensity, so it has no limit in its variety and depth and scope, and by the same token our own reflection of that love in our own lives.

All this applies with equal force to the situation of the aged, for least of all should the aged be unaware of the many angles and entrances open to them in their contact with the world force of love. Their own personal diminution is a pledge, in the divine economy, of the validity and power of the world force at their command.

The proverbial timidity of the aged can be a virtue, when it encourages us to be realistic as to the limited, diminished extent of our own powers. You are not a coward, nor are you some kind of a betrayer of high ideals, when in your latter years you frankly recognize that you have to make certain compromises with the physical and cultural world around you. The "foot of cogitation" must feel the ground more cautiously before it takes a giant step. But timidity is not a virtue, it is a vice, often a serious vice, when it is merely an excuse for selfishness. And selfishness can take aggressive, dynamic forms. Psychologists inform us that many of the meanest forms of vice, sexual and otherwise, have their origin in timidity.

Timidity can be cultivated by skillful manipulators of the human psyche. It can be whipped up into panic, one of the most powerful and degrading of human emotions. It's a delight to anybody who has an ounce of human feeling to watch those bouncing, little orphan babies in their cribs. I am sure there are few motherly ladies who wouldn't want to pick them up and just give the little ones an extra bounce. Yet the seeds of panic lie between them and a happy future. What might happen? What could happen? Good Lord, what would people say? What would happen to the family, or the community — if you should adopt one of them? The idea is desperately panicky, and panic spreads. Sooner or later those jolly babes will meet directly with its force; it will show its ugly face. The older citizens, oh yes, will be sympathetic, to a degree, a very safe degree, but the thought of advising people to go any further than this very cautious limit of safety — safe distance, safe dismissal of the whole matter as something for the public agencies to take care of; we pay taxes to support their very job — the thought of anything further makes any cautious person nervous. Better dismiss the matter, turn off the TV when it raises the question, live our own safe lives. We won't be around too long anyway, so if any "problem" does arise, the future generation can somehow take care of it. We are weak and have little strength at our disposal. Nothing at our command, but the power of the Infinite, the glory and might of the Eternal, at the disposal of every human being who turns to Him for aid in the agelong contest for human unity and social peace.

If the children of the vast world can be called upon

periodically to pray for the world's unity and peace, why cannot the aged show courage, and, with their experience and knowledge, urge the rest of the world to cast false timidity, groundless panic, to the winds. There are so many occasions when older people, by their words, reasoning, and example can encourage younger and stronger people to close their ears to panic, to "widen the spaces of their charity"; to make ventures even at the risk of some discomfort or possible disappointment; to take time and trouble to learn facts, not rumors and conjectures; to set their own pace at that of the Kingdom of God.

4. THE PRESENCE OF ETERNITY

My religious faith teaches me that the Creator has His own way of entering our lives and making Himself felt. Entering means giving new meaning to our lives. It means giving new meaning to our lives' various phases or epochs, one of which is the final epoch of old age. As we grow in our concept of love, in proportion to the tremendous growth of variety and complexity in the modern age, we discover new ways in which the Creator can make His entrance. There is no door that need be closed to Him, and we can encounter Him most intimately in our darkness and defeat.

There is no period of life, as long as we have reasonable exercise of our faculties, that we cannot continue to some degree to grow mentally. We may not be accumulating new facts, or developing new techniques and skills, but we certainly can enlarge our understanding of the world around us, whether of human beings or of things. Few occupations are more satisfying than that of rereading old classics; they take on a new meaning as we see them in the light of a life's experience. Age is the time for some degree of contemplation. I am not speaking of mental rapture, but rather of the thoughtful, peaceful enjoyment of nature, of art, of the sequence of human events, of insight into those relations and connections of things that so often means so much more than the individual objects themselves.

A good biography, for instance, that in earlier days wearied us by its references and details, speaks meaningfully to us in latter years. People we may have known personally, in public or private life, can tell an absorbing story when viewed in retrospect. Very simple things can speak deeply to us in those later years, somewhat as they spoke to us in early childhood: the mystery of ordinary occurrences, of day and night, of nature's lavish multiplicity, of its astounding complexity and vitality; the sea, the shore and the mysterious coves and inlets where the "infinite" ocean meets the land; the changing forest, the desert, the world of the sky and clouds. Poets and philosophers have written endlessly of these things, and presumably will continue to do so. Yet nature's moods and variations are always a surprise, and in later years you are surprised that they seem to have new meanings, often most where you least expect it.

Popular science, let us say astronomy, in the macrocosm,

or genetics, in the microcosm, is supposed, being popular, to be stuff for children: nice for them to get it in the formative years, but beneath your dignity later on, unless you can specialize. But isn't it the privilege of age precisely to *enjoy* the fruits of specialist toil? Quite incapable of mastering the intricate formulas of genetics, I can enjoy in my later years peering through the geneticist's microscope, and seeing how new living beings originate and take shape. In this way, I can contemplate certain phases of life itself.

We cannot love human beings without loving their institutions and traditions. We are not loving abstract beings, but men as citizens of the earth: as they are bound by economic needs and as they govern. We cannot truly love mankind, unless we respect the civilization that gave them dignity, the culture that evoked their talents, the discoveries that revealed in them a divine spark of intelligence.

Moralists distinguish between the claims of charity and justice; and for practical purposes it is necessary that they should do so. Yet in reality neither of these virtues can exist in complete independence of the other. Any attempt to establish such independence will ultimately break down at one point or the other.

In the Oriental paintings — Chinese or Japanese — you do not see young people seated in meditation near a waterfall. The contemplative hermit is aged, quite as a matter of course. This is age's prerogative, to be seated near the roaring stream of life, and relate it to the imperishable stream of one's own life within one.

Precisely in these latter days you become aware of a new life growing: with a freshness and vitality beyond the categories of other new experiences. You become aware of something that has been with you, very likely, since childhood — that you have loved and honored, yet comes to you now with new meanings. It speaks to you not of either past or present but of the future; or rather it doesn't speak to you in terms of time at all. Silently, unobtrusively, steadily (unless you deliberately thwart it), a new life grows within you: the presence of Him who is the Resurrection and the Life. It is none other than the birth and growth of divine charity: of love for God and man.

If given any freedom, given its logical course, this new life will invade your old life: will possess you, will *create* a new being within you. In old age, in other words, you become much less a record of what you have once been by your (bygone) efforts, as a record of what the Creator is working out within you: the birth of this new life, the life of the Resurrection, the life of Eternity. I am using eternity not in the merely negative sense of "having no end," but the positive sense of the presence to you and through you of the Eternal. For now life has found its *true* meaning. The meaning of age is the meaning of life itself: life as the workshop of the Creator, ever vivifying, perfecting, developing our own true selves within us.

The sign of this divine operation is the presence of charity: love of God and man, love seen as a gift, poured out in our hearts by the Spirit of God.

Love as a life, as a new life that flows to us from the Source of all life and power, is not conditioned by the general law of diminishment that characterizes our merely earthly life. No matter how much age may rob me of strength of body or mind, or of all the gifts that seem to make life meaningful, age cannot rob me of the power to share in the world-wide operation of God's love moving and stirring in this world. There is no condition of mind or body, in which I cannot in some way, in some fashion or manner, practice some form of love for God and man. Sickness, suffering, death itself can be offered up as a holocaust of love. At the time of this life's greatest weakness, I have at my disposal the exercise of a social dynamism, which exceeds in the long run any merely human force. I don't say that my individual action will manifest that force: it will pass unnoticed, save for the very few, or the chance individual, who may benefit by it. But it is known to God, it is part of His divine operation on earth, and as such it is part of His all-conquering enterprise. Once we begin to grasp this truth, we are surprised to see what a perspective it opens up to us.

Certainly, judged by merely material standards, age compels us to drop all sorts of the "good works" that have, perhaps, formed part of our biography. I cannot bustle and hustle any more; I have sent in my resignation; I have no "means" at hand to respond to daily pleas for help. I become more of a cipher, a mere item in a past record. Judged by *those* standards, my tangible love of neighbor is diminished to the point of extinction. But those are not the standards of God's operation, not the measure of the life of charity. On the contrary, there is no condition or circumstance, of body or soul, which I cannot glorify by some

[85]

act of love for my fellow human being, as long as the breath of life remains in me. Even if I am reduced to total helplessness, I can still offer my life as a holocaust in union with the Church's work throughout the world: offer up all that I have for the living and the dead.

And what an infinite variety of ways for the aged to practice, simply, tangibly, and effectively, the love of their neighbor once they begin to seek that opportunity! We can never do, never hope to do, a thousandth part of what we would *wish* to do. But the main thing is that we can always do *something*. Even if you are in jail, you may be able to lend a good book to the inmate of the next cell!

We are constantly being informed, by all the agencies that reach the eye and ear, how many disagreeable and depressing features blight our modern life. The modern world is impersonal and ruthless, destructive of human values and neighborliness. I shall not try to argue the point. Nevertheless, each of the unpleasant features of modern existence — in its civilized and in its uncivilized aspects — opens up occasions where the individual, and in particular the *aged* individual, can do something to help his or her fellow human being. Present circumstances create loneliness, granted. But other lonely people can be visited, and visiting lonely people — sick, in prison, what have you — is precisely one of those things that according to the Saviour will rate most at the Last Judgment.

The concept of love is not something just given us once and for all. Rather, it is a concept that develops, multiplies, transforms what has already been accomplished, in the way of serving and loving our neighbor, in the way of penetrating more and more deeply into the causes of human misery.

Love is continually defeated; hate, violence, deceit gain the upper hand. So many of the proposals for building a reign of peace and unity in the world turn out to be blind alleys; so often the remedy becomes even worse than the disease. Yet for all its difficulties and handicaps, love, seen in the fullness of its dimensions, remains an unconquerable force in human affairs.

5. CONTEMPLATION AND PRESENCE

By a curious turn of events — and I am not the first to comment upon this — these days of ever-multiplying activities in the public and private field and increasing claims on the individual's privacy, are also days of increasing stress upon the need of a contemplative element in our lives. Precisely the most active, responsible men and women, those most dedicated to their respective vocations or professions, seem most conscious of the need to enter into themselves from time to time in peace and quiet; they need time to reflect, to meditate, to ponder and savor the words of life: in short, to practice some form of contemplation.

Great spiritual writers, past and present, who urge contemplation, are in ever-increasing demand. People return as never before to reflect upon the words of the Scriptures, the acts and the language of the Saviour and His disciples, the mysterious utterances of the prophets and apostles.

[87]

Distinguished writers have discussed the privileges and methods of contemplation, of "consideration," as St. Bernard of Clairvaux called it and recommended its practice to the busy-burdened Pope Eugene IV. Here only would I say that old age is a time when we can read and ponder best upon the words of life given us in the Scriptures. The words take on new meanings, unlock doors that heretofore were barred by confusion and misunderstanding. We begin to see what our life is all about; what the Creator has made of us, and what He is trying to fashion in our minds and hearts.

I am not proposing permanent retirement to a monastery or the solitude of the desert, though there are few of us who do not benefit by such a temporary retirement. But in the latter years of life you will be richly rewarded if you can afford to enjoy a time of meditation or reflection. You can let much of the world go by; you can think more often and more affectionately of the new life that is being born within you. And you will return renewed to whatever tasks still await you. Yet you don't need a monastery in order to practice contemplation. The subway, the bus, or the Chicago elevated can be ideal for this purpose. One might establish a special order of subway contemplatives.

Contemplation will especially indicate to us the mysterious way God gives each of us a share in that infinite source of life from which we originated, and to which we are scheduled to return. That source is eternity.

People are afraid of the idea of eternity. The word itself discomforts them. It recalls Edgar Allan Poe, or tantalizing sermons about the clock with the immovable hour hand, forever pointing to an everlasting *now*. The word eternity seems to evoke the image of an intolerably oppressive amount of time, everlasting, changeless time, like a motionless landscape on the moon. If that is what eternity is, we are afraid to be caught by it, to be fixed in its fixity.

The reason for such a misunderstanding is plain enough. Eternity is a transcendental notion, which can be expressed only in negative terms. Our language can only state what eternity is *not*, that it does not contain the element of change, of before and after, in the sense of time progression. It is the divine Reality, of which our short times and long times are but a reflection. Of itself, eternity is none other than the infinitely loving and lovable God. It is God, as we might say, *under the duration aspect*: God as time declares Him, reveals Him, under the special aspect of duration.

If I conceive eternity merely as something that I predicate of God, it impresses me but does not warm me. Eternity, however, is not just a something, an abstraction, but is a Person, a Person Who *is* Eternity, just as He is Unity, Love, Omnipotence, Omnipresence. We talk in doctrinal terms about the attributes of God, we speak of God as having eternity, etc.; but Eternity *is* the Living God, is the Living Creator. When He speaks to me, or when He touches me, it is Eternity itself who speaks, or whom I touch.

God is not determined, as I am, by time, nor is He bound by time's categories. I cannot describe in terms of the calendar Him Whose "years do not fail." Yet since I am a time-bound being — immortal in one aspect, time-bound in another — I must talk of my Creator from the time aspect, as it were, from the aspect of "duration." And when I use that language, I speak of Him as the Eternal, I speak of Him as Eternity itself.

We are accustomed to think of eternity as a remote situation in the future, as something we shall somehow find a way to reconcile ourselves to when the moment comes for its arrival. Yet our faith teaches that eternity has already arrived; that it is already part of our present lives. We do not, it is true, sense its presence as we do the material or even the psychic world around us. We live, think, and act as if our experience were bounded by the ticking of the clock or the changes of the four seasons. Yet are we so totally unconscious of its presence? Even for the least imaginative of us there are moments when the transcendent God, Who *is* Eternity, as He is Immensity and Omnipotence, speaks to us in His own language, if we will have but the patience to listen.

T. S. Eliot, in his *Burnt Norton*, felt the presence of Eternity when he listened in the garden to the hidden laughter of little children. It was here, and now, and always. Eternity enters my life with every act of genuine love: of the child for its mother, of the spouses joined by the golden ring, of the aged for one another and for all humanity. And, as those unwanted orphan children bounce in their cribs I see the Eternal — Who Himself *is* Eternity — making His entrance upon the scene and offering the gift of His own life — a life which *is* Eternity — to those of us who have the courage to accept it, and say *Amen.*

The doors of power that are opened to me in my old age,

so many doors, so much power-through-weakness, are no less than the many ways in which the Living Eternal enters into my time-sphere. He enters not as a stranger, not as one foreign to all that I am and experience. Rather, at His entrance, I find myself the meaning of my inmost self; I find that Reality for which my entire life is an expectation.

An artist, in his own way, may help us to see these mysterious truths with a little more clarity. The artist's personages fix the restlessness of our discursive minds.

Many years ago, a young American painter paused before one of Rembrandt's paintings, one that represented the moment when the Saviour broke bread at Emmaus with Cleophas and his companion disciple. Wrote the painter in later years:[2]

It was reserved for Rembrandt to give us both the fact and the mystery. The little painting in the Louvre, which I remember as shabby, is notwithstanding one of the greatest pictures in the world, and we feel, as I say, that his Bible is *the* Bible. The story shows us the recognition, as if we were there. There is the disciple who, recognizing, joins his hands in prayer; the other stops in astonishment, placing his napkin before him and gazes at the Christ; the boy sees nothing as he brings a plate.

They are of earth, and properly and rightly — but the central figure has passed through Death. He is alive, and yet — a little breath, a slight look, make all the difference.

"O foolish and slow of heart," He had upbraided them, as He walked with the two anxious disciples in the Pales-

[2] J. LaFarge, *The Gospel Story in Art*, Macmillan, 1925, p. 403.

tinian countryside, and had explained to them how the new and imperishable life was to come to them through the suffering, rejection, and death of the Son of God. "O foolish and slow of heart . . ."

When it's all over and we look back at our old age as we now look back at our earlier life, we may apply these same words to ourselves and wonder why it was that *we* did not see the risen life already operating with us during the hours of darkness or suffering. The moments when that life is most evident were those when we imparted a bit of it, through love, to our neighbor. In those moments we are joined, as it were, with the countless people in God's Kingdom who are lighting the torch of the Resurrection.

Time is an old acquaintance after all. We are used to its vagaries, the oddest of which is its practical disappearance for several hours out of the twenty-four. We can capture it, put it under a certain degree of control by our elaborate system of timekeeping, from the calendar and hourglass to the atomic clock. But we don't know, or at least cannot *imagine* to ourselves, a timeless existence. Yet eternity, as such is positive. The eternity pledged to by divine hope is the *fullness* of duration; that reality; that present-ness for which our whole being longs, toward which we instinctively and perpetually strive.

When eternity does "arrive" our deepest feeling will be: this is where I am at home. This is the reality, the self-realization, which I have been seeking, consciously or unconsciously, all my life. This is what I have sensed; have touched, in a way, by the subtlest antennae of my mind, at unexpected turns of the road during my time-pilgrimage.

The Power of Love

When I first come in sensible contact with the risen life, I shall realize with lucid clarity what I now know only by faith, and the reasoning that deduces from faith. I shall perceive immediately and vividly that the moments in my life that seemed most contrary to hope, the moments of humiliation, and of depression, of sheer tedium, when hope seemed farthest away . . . these were those instants in which the solidity, the firmness of hope, was closest and most tangible.

The moments when I faced fear and conquered it, trusting in divine hope, were the moments when I felt more deeply the reality of the divine promise. This is the lesson in God's dealings with mankind in all times and circumstances. It is the *way:* certain, unfailing, but inexplicable.

When the peace of eternity finally touches us, we shall recall the moments of agony, of doubt, in our lives, and see how God's hope was then sustaining us. But we shall also recall the dead moments, the times of weariness, routine, petty disappointments, and see the great pattern of eternity being worked out in those moments as well. You may meet God in the convent chapel, or meet His presence on the battlefield, or in the downtown office or the classroom. You may meet Him most intimately when the harsh alarm clock sounds off in the morning, and you face once more the sheer burden of daily routine. But if you seek Him, you will find Him. And you will meet Him most palpably in the Garden of Olives and on Calvary.

Part IV

SOCIETY'S RESPONSIBILITY

I have spoken of old age as a personal problem; one that affects each of us without exception. But old age concerns us also as a social problem; one that affects our society at every angle. You cannot discuss employment, any form of business or labor organization, any aspect of family life or marriage, trade, travel, politics, without running into intricacies created by the aging of citizens, men and women. No amount of wishful thinking can free us from pondering the questions raised by old age.

Today, in our modern world, the absence of certain modern comforts is a cruel hardship, and the same would apply to deprivation of milk, bread, ordinary cooking and laundering facilities, etc. It is not, as I see it, the will of our Father in Heaven that the world's natural progress should be enjoyed by any one people, race, group, or age. Moreover, such deprivations are apt to be more cruel in the latter years than in the prime of life. When the elevator sticks, younger tenants can manage to walk up; for the senior citizens the stoppage of the elevator, *in an elevator-functioning culture,* can be close to a death sentence. Charitable and energetic Pope John found himself a bit out of breath when at Christmas-time, 1962, he climbed some

[97]

steep stairs in order to visit and bless the children in an institution for juvenile delinquents.

In the world at large, the proportion of aged men and women who are tormented by the most elementary types of want — the lack of even the bare essentials of nourishment, clothing, medicine, etc. — is usually very much greater than our imagination can conceive. Our tourist folders don't elaborate this aspect of foreign travel. If the folders pictured the situation familiar to any parish priest or social worker within ten minutes' walk of that magnificent million-dollar hotel, the description would offer an interesting background to your trip. Yet satirical remarks make little practical sense. Better to remember that the million-dollar hotel does, in point of fact, provide work and sales opportunity for large numbers of local people who would otherwise be destitute. We also pray that among the hotel's guests some will do serious thinking as to what their own country can do to aid the distress of the economically backward countries.

To be borne in mind is the sobering situation that right here in our own prosperous United States we still have so much of what Michael Harrington calls *The Other America*; the "invisible" multitudes of the poor and among them, most of all, the aged poor.[1]

However much one may argue about this or that formulation of rights, or any particular measure aiding to implement them, vindication of the rights of the aged stands out as an essential part of our civilization. To love the old

[1] M. Harrington, *The Other America*, Macmillan, 1962, p. 104.

[98]

people benevolently without any particular regard for their basic rights — as persons and specifically as aged individuals and members of a family — may accomplish many good deeds and relieve, through sheer kindness, many forms of misery. But as long as this display of kindness is a mere favor to one's fellow human being and not the fulfillment of a serious claim, it will leave the deeper issues untouched. On the other hand, no matter how finely carpentered is our structure of correlative rights and duties, if love is absent from their implementation, if those who exercise this responsibility are not conscious of their high office as ministers of the Creator's love to their own fellow creatures — if this divinely motivated element is lacking — in the long run what is done becomes a mere mechanical function, as odious to the recipient as it is uninspiring to the agents themselves. No matter how scientifically the structure of old-age care may be patterned, if its aim is merely the abstract welfare of the body politic, the beneficiary of such welfare remains a mere object for the functioning of the public weal: a hateful situation for men or women approaching the final term of their lives. As in private intercourse, so too in public institutions, the test of reality — as opposed to gilded mockery — is that subtle touch that convinces the recipients of care and kindness that they are loved, not as mere derelicts to be peacefully disposed of by whatever inoffensive means are possible, but as our own brothers and sisters in the great march of traveling humanity. They are dear to us, and honored by us, because they are close to the goal toward which we are all hastening.

The genuine *home* for older people is clearly differentiated from the mere justitution by precisely this personal touch, this recognition of innate dignity: guests, not "inmates." It makes little difference whether the aged are institutionalized or still living in private residence, such a recognition of individual personality, even in rather simple, casual form, can mean the differences between blank diffidence, and even despair, and the warm nourishment of a spark of human hope. A striking example of what can be done in this respect, in quite original fashion, is the visiting service of the Little brothers of the poor (absence of capital letters is intentional on their part) an offshoot of Père Marquiset's Petits frères des pauvres in France. They operate on the principle that nothing is too precious, too select for the aged poor, and they are visited and treated like the most intimate and honored guests.

The Senate Report of the 1961 White House Conference on Aging drew up a succinct statement under the name of the SENIOR CITIZEN'S CHARTER, ON THE RIGHTS AND OBLIGATIONS OF OUR SENIOR CITIZENS. The statement goes beyond the cold cataloguing of social facts, and places in a moral framework the question of society's responsibility toward the aged, and its correlative, their own responsibility, which cannot be passed over to the rest of the national community. Under the heading of rights, each of our senior citizens, regardless of race, color, or creed, is entitled to a multitude of the same: to be useful, to obtain employment, to be free from want, etc.

To its statements and recommendation on the social problems of the aged, the Senate Committee added a brief statement on religion, remarks which have added significance, in view of the discussions that have taken place since then regarding the position of religion in our public schools. The introductory paragraph reads as follows and coincides with the basic philosophy of this book:

"The meaning of life is to be found solely in man's relationship to God. It is this relationship which gives meaning to all human values. In the light of it, every period of life, including that of old age, is possessed of intrinsic value and sublime potential. Viewed in the light of an eternal destiny, old age is seen to have an importance as great as that of youth or the middle years. To young and old, the divine imperative is addressed: 'Thou shalt love the Lord thy God . . . and thy neighbor as thyself.'"

So that religion may play its full and proper part in the life of the aging, it is recommended that care be exercised to provide suitable transportation and facilities for participation in worship, and services and congregations. In order to reach the shut-ins, greater use should be made of religious radio, TV, and recordings, as well as the personal ministries of members and leaders. It is urged also, that state, county, and municipal governments recognize the need for more chaplain's services in public institutions caring for the aging. Ways of providing such services should be studied on local, state, and national levels by religious bodies and public agencies.

The most difficult core problem of the old-age social question is the problem of extreme poverty. Where poverty sets in, all the natural difficulties of old age are alarmingly compounded and interacting. This interaction works either way you care to express it. When people are poor, downright poor and really destitute, then the normal inconveniences of old age become alarming. They plummet into despairing misery. They must put up with inferior, often decayed, ramshackle housing. In this modern age, lack of proper heating facilities, poor lighting, and wretched sanitation are coupled with crowding and deprivation of decent privacy. Physical handicaps, like crippling rheumatic disorders or impaired sense perceptions or circulatory disorders, present difficulties enough under favorable circumstances. But when age is accompanied by poverty, the condition becomes a nightmare. If no possibility of physical therapy is available, a condition that normally is annoying but tolerable becomes a menace. At the same time, the distress of the aged poor is easily exploited by hostile elements in our society; by criminal agencies; and by certain types of political practitioners.

In his vigorous presentation of the amount of real poverty that prevails even in our prosperous United States, Michael Harrington remarks that leisure itself can be a burden to the destitute aged.

Loneliness, isolation, and sickness are the affliction of the aged in every economic class. But for those who are poor, each of these tragedies is intensified; they are more lonely, more isolated, sicker. So it is that a Government report unwillingly stated a social paradox. It noted that only a society of abundance could produce such a high proportion of old people. We can afford them, we create them because we are so rich. But later, in discussing the reality of life for the aged, the same report noted that these human products of abundance were denied its fruits. We tolerate them as long as they are poor.

The 1960 Senate Report stated the issue clearly enough: ". . . at least one-half of the aged — approximately eight million people — cannot afford today decent housing, proper nutrition, adequate medical care, preventative or acute, or necessary recreation." The same grim picture emerged from the White House Conference on Aging in 1961. As one volume put it: "Many states report that half their citizens over 65 years have incomes too low to meet their basic needs."

Nothing is more striking than the contrast between the misery of the homeless and neglected aged in the midst of a highly developed civilization, and the example of what can be done by intelligent and loving care to make life reasonably comfortable, reasonably significant, and productive as well.

Writes Maya Pines in *The Reporter* for May 10, 1962:

No amount of legislation alone can cope with the staggering problems raised by growing numbers of old people who, because of chronic disease or mental deterioration, have become unable to fend for themselves.

For the sick aged and their families, the facts of life are brutal. The period of acute illness, with its high medical and hospital bills, is only the starting point of a long and increasingly difficult journey. A whole family's life savings of $10,000 can easily disappear in well-meant but inade-

[103]

quate care at home, or in payments to a poorly staffed commerical nursing home—after which the elderly patient may be permanently bedridden and his family broke.

The best-known facilities for the aged, remarks the same author, are the commercial nursing homes whose patients average eighty years of age. Yet despite their tremendous growth, no real supervision of commercial nursing homes exists. The trouble with the nonprofit institution for the aged has been that few of them tried to help older people who were "not ill enough to stay in the hospital yet too ill to be cared for properly in their own homes: the 'non-ill.'" However, in recent times "some of the best nonprofit homes for the aged have quietly started what may amount to a revolution in the treatment of the aged." Not only have they set up first-rate infirmaries for people who fall ill after admittance, but also in the past few years many have begun to accept old people who are quite ill. Sometimes these are admitted directly upon discharge from a hospital or a mental hospital.

A lifelong student of the problem, Mother M. Bernadette de Lourdes, O. Carm., Superior, Home for the Aged in Bridgeport, Connecticut, remarks that many of the problems peculiar to the older people of our own day arise from the fact that neither our attitude nor our social programs have fully kept pace with the changed times. "We are, as it were, in midstream. Grandparents are as important in the total scheme of life, but their social and psychological value has been in part obscured, diminished, and confused by the conflicts and uncertainties of a transitional period."

The attitude of Catholic institutions, Mother Bernadette says, has undergone many changes during the past twenty-five years. In the past, the institution for the aging was regarded as a place in which one prepared for death. Today our Catholic homes are behives of activity in which the aging live more normally and happily. This has been accomplished in great part through the utilization of community resources in conjunction with the services given in the homes.

Says the same author:

The more progressive homes for the aging have many facilities which were unheard of twenty-five years ago. The staff consists of teams of physicians, dentists, podiatrists, speech therapists, laboratory and X-ray technicians, dietitians, social workers, recreational directors, occupation therapists and others. To assist the medical staff in making more speedy and accurate diagnoses many homes have made available clinical laboratories, diagnostic X-ray facilities, and other equipment such as basal metabolism and electrocardiograph machines. Over and above the regular staff, consultants in all medical activities, advisers in the field of social service, creative activities and recreational programs for the elderly give their valuable advice and encouragement so that the aging may enjoy their harvest years to the fullest. . . . Counseling may well spell the difference between an old age spent in resignation of a hard fate and

[105]

old age spent in constructive usefulness to self and others.[2]

Much, very much, can be said and written about the irony of the poverty situation in this country, especially as it affects the aged poor. A classic factor is the impact of automation; the more that labor is saved by the skill and ingenuity of inventive science, the more people are deprived in their declining years of moderately useful employment. Those of us who have had any kind of rural background can recall the variety of useful jobs, indoors and outdoors, that older people could do upon the farm: such matters as the care of smaller livestock, preparation of meals, various types of cleaning and repairs, watching over small children, etc. Modern conveniences, the kind of apparatus you purchased from Sears and Roebuck, eased a lot of troubles. The aged tenant farmer, who had plodded under the hot sun behind his fly-tormented team for a good part of his near eighty years, could now continue his work with a "riding plow," not a luxurious contrivance, it is true, but still one that enabled him to keep the rickety old home, while he let his sons exchange their farm work for more lucrative jobs. In later days, when grandfather had gone to his well-earned repose, new, high-power machinery offered its expert services to the younger generation. If the "new farmer" could make good, the new apparatus was a blessing. But if the costs and intricacies of the new farm economy got the better of him, Grandpa was gently but firmly set on the road for the enjoyment of whatever hospitality society

[2] *The Catholic Church and Social Welfare.* Marguerite T. Boylan, Editor. Greenwich Book Publishers, 489 Fifth Avenue, New York 17, N.Y. 1962, pp. 80–99.

could show for the aged poor. Nobody in his senses would want to return to those early and picturesque times, so pleasant for the aged in some respects, so miserable and intolerable when crippling sickness struck. Nonetheless, modern progress still exacts a harsh toll, just when you think it has most eased the burden of life.

Yet it would be entirely foolish to give the problem up as insoluble. It is not the absolute fact of progress that creates so much misery; it is the uneven pace, the complication with so much ignorance in those who administer it, the extreme inequalities of its impact upon totally differing cultures and classes, and, last but not least, the callousness of our own consciences in facing the moral problems that every advance toward greater unity and prosperity carries in its train.

It would be an impertinence on my part to try to present a "solution" of so interlaced a situation as that in which I find a surprisingly large number of my old fellow citizens entangled. This would be the work of an expert and a social strategist. But what I can do, and what seems to me is imperative upon any honest citizen under these circumstances, is to suggest a couple of simple requirements for reaching any viable pathway out of the woods. If we have some idea of where we are going, we are more liable to find the way. Hence I propose the following considerations:

First, *clarity as to the goal.* We are not attempting to abolish old age. I don't mean abolishing it as a time-phenomenon, which I leave to the future cosmonauts, but even abolishing it as a necessary phase of life. Unless we move into an entirely different dispensation, of which I see neither likelihood nor possibility, old age will always be laden with a certain degree of personal diminishment, often of personal discomfort. But there is no reason why we cannot continue to lessen progressively for old age those miseries, — sufferings, isolation, depression — which do not necessarily attach to it, even in the exile under which the human race now lives. To take a homely example. Fifty years ago it appeared necessary, from the very nature of the case, for all but a possible privileged few among the aged to be quite cut off from a pleasant conversation with their friends and neighbors once a degree of deafness set in. If their eyesight failed, they had no resources except to be read to by some obliging friend or relative. Long flights of stairs, primitive wheel chairs — if they enjoyed even that much convenience — awkward sanitary facilities plagued their daily lives; they still plague the lives of thousands. Yet the various facilities for alleviating these annoyances are at hand, if we can but find the ways and means for their acquisition and distribution. If it is our aim to enable the aged to enjoy each other's company and the company of their younger citizens, if we have in mind the planning and organizing of a fuller and richer life, sooner or later, barring some unforeseen catastrophe, we can surely discover the way thither.

Second, *clarity as to responsibility.* Fundamental to any solution of the plight of the aged poor is to settle without shadow of doubt the responsibility of society towards the aged, and the many varieties and ramifications of that responsibility. In the civic field, the national government carries a responsibility, as is frankly acknowledged by the Senate Committee's inquiry, previous to proposed legislation. But the Federal government's action is frustrated, whether it be Medicare or some other plan, unless it is supported by a sense of responsibility at every level of human association: the states, the town or municipal units, voluntary and especially church units and organizations.

The young, especially when they begin to notice a little the flight of time, cannot avoid putting to themselves some questions as to how they will eventually fare. If they are of the conscientious type, they can hardly avoid the question: what is my responsibility toward the aged? What can I *now* do about the situation? And if they are in any way concerned about public affairs, they will naturally ask: is the present phenomenal increase of the aged a calamity, whether you speak in terms of absolute numbers or of a percentage of the entire population?

For that increase is an elementary fact.

None of us can be casual about the new developments as a result of the dramatic progress in life expectancy and in technology allowing increasing proportions of older folks to retire for more years than in the past. Today the average life expectancy in the United States is around 70 years. In 1900, it was less than 50 years. In the lifetime of today's young generation, without any further progress in medical science an average life expectancy of 80–85 will be typical. Even today there are 1 million Americans aged 85 and over. In fact, the segment of the nearly 17 million persons aged 75 or more increased 60 per cent since the 1950 census — the fastest growing part of our country's population.[3]

[3] Senate Report of the White House Conference on Aging, 1961.

If we read the record of the earliest Christian communities, as mentioned in the Acts of the Apostles and their various Epistles, we are struck by the thoroughness and loving care with which provision was made for the senior members of the community, men and women, and the several responsibilities entrusted to their members. For Christians today, one of the richest fruits of a revived consciousness of the subtle doctrine of the Mystical Body of Christ, the fruit of the extension of this doctrine into every branch of the Christian community, is, or should be, the sense of community with our senior members, a truly passionate desire to bring them into close association with their fellows and to conquer the specter of enforced isolation. Not only physical isolation is a barrier, such as one meets with so frequently in any of our large cities, but still more mental and spiritual loneliness. It is not just the question of being alone, physically or socially, but of feeling alone. For the old person, trapped in the decaying central area of the city and living among strangers, there is a terrifying lack of human contact.

Responsibility toward the aged cannot ignore the responsibilities of the aged themselves: to the rest of society, and to one another. It is part of at least this writer's credo that nothing is accomplished toward the relief of human misery, the nourishment of human hopes, without communicative intercourse between the unlike members or groups in the community, and a co-operative form of action to which such intercourse gives rise. Where these twin elements are absent, talk of mutual charity is apt to evaporate into the thin air of hypocrisy.

Society's Responsibility

If our aim is clear, and if our responsibilities are sharply defined, we are in a position to battle with and to conquer the enlaced evils that beset the aged poor in our supposedly blessed world of prosperity and civilization.

When people are old and are in acute distress, they do not want lectures on social theory. They want immediate help: food, lodging, medical or psychiatric care. Chronic disease is the greatest disability of the aged person. Yet when you encounter new instances of distress, you begin to realize how little your stopgap efforts count, unless attention is paid to the social order as a whole. Unfortunately it usually takes hard-luck cases to arouse us to the ills that afflict our society. The woman in the Bible had to tell the King of Israel she had killed, boiled, and eaten her own child before the King could realize the horrible situation famine had created in his own domain (2 Kings 6:25–31). In our own society, we need to be shaken up from time to time by certain startling discoveries so that we may finally get our minds working on the reconstruction of the social order.

Problems of old age, and of poverty-afflicted old age in particular, are closely linked. The complicated *economic* order under which we live; how we employ ourselves, for instance, and how we do and can make use of our leisure time. Leisure is attracting an increasing amount of attention these days, particularly as a spiritual problem and challenge, and has formed the theme of some of the best writing of the German philosopher, Josef Pieper. Our attitude toward leisure and the occupations with which we implement our leisure hours and our retirement is associated with the concept of our responsibility for the goods of the earth in general, whether they be our own personal gifts or the material and spiritual goods that surround us.

The situation of the aged, and particularly of the aged poor, is also part and parcel of the international order and the general situation of the human race as such. Many of the lonely, some of them near-destitute old people who live right in our own city neighborhood are here because the Iron Curtain blocks their access to their own Eastern European or in some cases Asiatic homeland. In our own country, how much of this situation is the result of migration, either immigration from abroad, or in-migration within our own political confines?

Problems of mass movements within our population immediately involve matters like location of the dispossessed. What will become of you when you are suddenly bounced out of your fairly decent and comfortable brownstone apartment, and left stranded — presumably for the time being, but stranded nonetheless — while the real estate speculators are making up their minds as to the type of people for whom their next apartment project will be built? Will it be for your relatively meager $30, or will it be in the $70 or $80 class? And so on. And what are you supposed to do about it? What can aged citizens do about it, while life is still left within them to meet and talk and propose? How are the younger generation being trained to observe and come now to the aid of the older folk, and to prepare for their own eventualities later when the number of people to be housed may have increased astronomically? And is the thorny problem of population increase to be left to propagandists and not treated with the apparatus of scholarly scientific research that it deserves?

Those of us who have known what it is to live and function in a simpler, less highly organized world will view with disturbance the ever more highly rationalized intricacies of our modern existence. We are troubled that so many great inventions bring added burdens in their train. Automation frees men from dull, repetitive tasks, says the British scientist and mathematician, L. J. Bronowski,[4] and places at man's disposal, through nuclear energy, the mechanical equivalent of twenty slaves a year. But these fruits of man's intelligence are still woefully maldistributed. We are still far from a "worldwide cooperation that permits and favors an orderly and fruitful international exchange of useful knowledge, capital and manpower."[5]

Despite these difficulties however, aged people in our own time may recover some of the privileged positions they enjoyed in earlier and simpler periods. They will doubtless be pushing IBM levers and buttons because there will be so many buttons and levers to push, so many more opportunities to use a minimum of physical effort or psychic strain, coupled with added opportunity for experienced judgment and responsibility. In the total running of things, less may be left to the imagination and initiative of youth; there will be more room and more responsibility connected with old age. I am not saying this is altogether a good

4 New York *Times Magazine*, July 15, 1962.
5 *Mater et Magistra*, No. 192.

thing. Aged hands at times may throw the wrong switches, and the panic button is surprisingly easy at hand for them to manipulate. Yet the development of new employment opportunities, suitable for a complexified age, seems to be normal.

Take the mere matter of collecting and collating data and literary references: a task which is bound to grow in density and importance as the mass of printed, and otherwise recorded, material increases. Who will be preparing all that material? Will more and more young people be buried in reference libraries? Or can much of the handling, ordering, winnowing of this collective mass of information and productive creation be entrusted to the older citizens? Entrusted, that is to say, in quite a common-sense way: in surroundings and with facilities geared to their condition, both physically and psychologically. Is this just an old man's dream, or is it a possibility? Here our senior librarians can speak, no longer just custodians of the great libraries of our increasingly complex modern life. For we may well find that if the old do not come to our rescue in sorting and classifying the mountains of acquired erudition, we shall be swamped, with the interpretive burden resting upon our youth.

Parallel with a social restatement, we can welcome a spiritual restatement as well. The dimensions of love offer ever-new fields for showing one's love for God and man. In the somber complexity of the new-fashioned world, truth itself, simple factual truth, grows in value. There is extreme need today for those courageous individuals who will speak from personal knowledge of the past, so easily forgotten or even barely intelligible to a younger generation. Should the brief space of twenty years be allowed to obliterate the memory of the once-independent nations of Poland, Hungary, Lithuania, Latvia, Estonia, Bulgaria? Yet if the elders do not speak, how will the past be kept from utterly perishing? What of Russia itself, and the precious record of the intelligence and great reform movements that existed before the Soviet revolution? Lives will be found of men and women who will consecrate themselves in special fashion to the separation of the true from the false; to the preservation and evaluation of records that will, in their turn, be a guide and inspiration for future ages. The historical-minded among us regret there were not more of such truth-seeking and fact-seeking minds in the past, say at the beginning of our American colonies. Can we not today perform these services for future generations? Self-interest can make us say: what has the future generation done for me, that I should toil in its behalf? But love cannot speak that way, for love's dimensions cover not only space, but all time as well.

Retirement can take on new meaning in a time when a certain life span does not so necessarily or naturally imply incapacity for great public service as it did before. Of course you don't learn very much by the example of evidently quite unusual people, who carry into extreme age a vitality that would be our envy at any time of life. Nevertheless, when at the date of this writing, Roscoe Pound, former dean of the Harvard Law School, finds it possible and rewarding at the age of 91 to spend full working hours each weekday at his old office, and even Saturdays from 9 A.M.

[115]

to 1 P.M., you wonder if there will not be more of this vitality as the fruit of increased *livableness* for the elder citizens. And with it, a new concept of spiritual opportunities.

The political aptitudes of the aging population offer so many possibilities, they give rise to so much speculation, that I do not dare to venture upon them. Harold L. Sheppard, of the Special Committee on Aging of the United States, expressed in an address to the annual meeting of the American Sociological Association, St. Louis, September 2, 1961, the idea that political movements among the aged may take new forms in the future, in spite of the advantages now offered by Social Security. "The thinking of this question," said Mr. Sheppard, "blows hot and cold, and much of it is tempered by a variety of conflicting wishes concerning the topic, and by a surprising influence of over-generalized stereotypes among even social scientists about the aged." There are still a great variety of ways in which the older citizens can make their influence felt, through party organizations, through special pressure groups, through information as to the attitudes of political candidates, etc. "Given the constant increases in longevity," says Sheppard, "how does this affect such phenomena as leadership succession and the circulation of elites in various types of organizations? 'Presidency for life' in the second half of the 20th century can mean something altogether different than it did at the beginning of this century — for an executive vice president or a junior executive with his status aspirations." And, in turn, developments in this line are affected by changes in the status of the family and the local community.

There is nothing in our modern, complexified, interacting civilization which of *itself* is either hospitable or inhospitable to old age. The "new world" can be completely friendly and homelike, or it can be bitterly unkind and spiritually desolate, not by any particular fault or virtue of its own, but according to the spirit which we put into it. We cannot create a heaven on earth for the aged, but we can make life livable, desirable, and profitable for them, if we love and cherish our fellow human beings. Or our beautiful new world can develop into a lonely, desolate place of individual exiles. It's a grand thing to provide hearing aids for the aged, once deafness puts in its appearance. After you get used to a certain amount of clatter and banging, hearing aids can delight you. They enable you to join in the conversations you have been so unpleasantly cut off from, and you get used to the accompanying din. But if the conversation itself is indifferent and hostile, what use is this particular bit of machinery? Like all other contrivances, it is an aid to human intercourse, but only the loving will of your fellow human being can *create* the acceptable interchange of knowledge, emotion, and ideas.

No magic formula will readily rid us of the tangled problems of old-age poverty. Yet there is no physical or moral necessity for misery. The Creator indeed wishes humankind to remember that they are creatures, that they are now living upon earth, and not in heaven, and that the human race in its present existence always bears the burden of a certain degree of punishment for its primal fall. Yet it is

[117]

His will that men seek rational means to improve their lot, and that the exercise of those same rational means of self-improvement can today, as always, become a hymn of praise to the Creator. Only a twisted mind can subscribe to the idea that in order to live as God wishes all His children to live, you have to deny His existence, and set up as an idol the blind forces of history.

No matter how efficiently and completely we clear out from old age all those annoyances and discomforts which normally attach to it, it still remains a time of waiting, not of complete fulfillment. Enlightened by faith, transformed by divine hope, it is a reminder that the entire human race, until the triumph of the Resurrection, is still in a certain state of punishment, which terminates only in death. Yet the character, the impact of this inherent punishment is changed, if it is accepted in all humility; if our lives say *Amen* to its unfolding, through the course of our final years, an unfolding which is never the same in any two individuals. The fact of this cosmic state of punishment does not in any way prohibit or interfere with every effort that we may make to alleviate our present condition, or to prepare for the final transformation in the end, of our personal selves and of the entire world.

The cosmos itself has not sinned even though the Evil One has tried to make it his playground. On the contrary, the cosmos in all its indescribable complexity, is God's work, endowed with its own intrinsic laws of development and growth, infinitely productive, infinitely subtle and dynamic in its age-long progression toward a goal in the future that we can only guess at, reasoning from what has been accomplished in the past. It is man who has sinned, and brought his share of disorder into the world, seduced by powers of evil which did not make the world, and whom the Creator will not suffer to unmake it, however they may perturb the present order. *How far these forces will triumph*, how far the quiet, myriad-fold work of ages will be promoted or will be frustrated — even for centuries, if certain demonic forces are allowed to have their way — depends on what man himself decides during the short time of his individual appearance here on earth. The value, the efficacy of that choice, depends not only upon the existence, but also upon the dimensions of man's love for God and mankind. For the least spark of that love is a mortal blast to the Evil One, the spirit of disorder and negation.

Part V

COURAGE IN OLD AGE

Were I to single out the quality that I should consider most important for old age, I would say it is courage.

To say that old people need courage, and need it *because* they are old, is to run counter to a lot of accepted ideas. It was Plato, I believe, who said in one of his crankier moments that the paramount traits of old age were wisdom and cowardice.

Certainly, it's easy enough to slip into a pusillanimous state of mind. With age, not only physical or muscular strength decreases, but one's psychic strength as well: the power to react promptly and intelligently to ordinary stimuli. You don't know just what people are saying, and you suspect the worst. So many new and unexpected dangers threaten, though for some unexplained reason, in New York City — I haven't checked on this for other places — the more decrepit aged people are, the greater risk they seem to enjoy taking in crossing the streets on foot against the traffic and the red light.

If aged people have courage, they themselves will help the society around them to find the ways and means to make aged life useful, profitable, and, relatively, congenial. Tranquilizing pills, of various descriptions, can relieve age of a few of its pains and discomforts. But only a few, only to a limited degree. I don't know who that fourth doctor is who turns up most every night on television as being cool to a certain type of pain remover that the other three so heartily endorse. Quite likely, he has no objection to the harmless remedy in question, but he just doesn't like to see people habitually resorting to chemical remedies when a brisk walk around the block and a little change in the diet would produce the same happy result. And very likely he's afraid of the pill habit, that can victimize the aged as it can victimize pregnant women. The courage to face a little discomfort here and now can often spare people great misery in the long run. However, that's a bit of hygiene. The soul-doctor is in no position to offer medical advice.

Allowing for all differences and normal precautions, there is nothing nobler in old age than true courage: nothing commands greater respect, as long as it *is* courage, and not just senile obstinacy. Age, by convention, is spared many of the rude shocks of youth; but by the same token, if we want to find its true meaning, it must be glorified by the type of courage which is in its own right, and suits its own condition.

The question of courage can be summed up in two words: the courage to *live*, and the courage to *love*. Said more precisely: the courage to accept our natural life, whatever be its length or circumstances, and the courage to accept the divine life, the life of the Resurrection, which is love.

The courage to live. My life is a gift, no matter what its conditions and circumstances. It can be full of misfortunes, it can be charged with bitter disappointments, it may have been willfully misspent; but nonetheless it is a gift, and, as long as I live, I can thank God for it. I thank Him each day, and if I wish to offer Him, the Author of life, the perfect thanks, I will do so by joining with my brethren in the sacrifice of thanksgiving, the Eucharist itself.

"I am waiting for the end to come, and the sooner the better," said to me a great and noble soul — incidentally in apparent health, and with all his faculties of intelligence, a keen esthetic appreciation, and a friendly relationship with all the world around him. "I believe I've done my work, and all I ask now of the good Lord is to take me away." Well that's the way he feels, and you can't argue with feelings. Yet to me his words did not quite make sense. Life is still a gift, it is an infinitely precious gift as long as you can still speak, or think or say Amen.

As long as I am *conscious*, master to any extent of my own world of inner choices, as long as in some way I can adore God and praise Him and thank Him, life is a gift. As long as I can suffer, for it is the strange prerogative of our humankind to suffer: that is to say, to know that we are suffering and to offer it as a mysterious gift to the Author of life, knowing by faith that suffering is the portal to life, life is a gift. The Venus rocket, which left Cape Canaveral in October 1962, reports from its (comparatively) near inspection of our companion planet conditions of such appalling heat, enough to melt lead, as would preclude the existence of any living being, and therefore of any creature that can suffer, much less be conscious of its own suffering.

Whether any such life possibility may exist on Mars remains still a pure speculation.

If we are truly grateful for the gift of life, we shall value the gift in new and unexpected ways. For we shall learn that life, as it is given us by the Creator, bears within itself the power of reparation, making amends for its own delinquencies. It has the power, through His grace and mercy, of re-creating itself. The mathematical discovery of relativity can *in theory* enable a person to live a year's time in a single month, if you are traveling at something like 99.5 per cent of the speed of light. But relativity cannot mend the past. Reparation is God's gift to us time-bound mortals. We can exercise it each day, each moment, that we simply and honestly thank Him for the mere gift of being alive.

The past, though it cannot be relived, can always be repaired. There is no mistake, no error, however radical and disastrous, however much shame and guilt it may have brought into our lives, that cannot be repaired by the healing power of that new life that is promised for our future, and, in the form of the living force of love, is given us here in this world. We can make reparation for our own sins and negligences, and for those of others. Moreover, we can join together in this work, and the aged of the entire world can join with all humanity in making this reparation. The presence and fulfillment, or the neglect and absence of such reparation — individual or common — can often determine the course of history. Can we not now, all of us, of whatever faith, race, or nationality, join in a sincere reparation for the bitter wounds inflicted upon the entire human race by past sins of division, resentment, and hatred?

This emphatically does not mean condoning present injustices. The captive nations of eastern Europe, like certain parts of the world still afflicted by racial injustices, cry out for liberation. But if we, the older folk of the world, join forces in humble offering of our old age and its burden, with the prayer that such present injustices be healed, and past injustices be atoned for, the reign of peace and justice may come more rapidly than we imagine.

If we have the courage to live — to accept each day as it is given to us, in all simplicity and humility — we shall find the way to carry out the chief acceptance of all: that of the end of life, of death. For what use is it to accept life, if you cannot accept that to which life leads?

The Church of God leads up to this somber, but not gloomy, truth in a very human way, with her daily evening prayer or Compline. In a succession of images Compline blends the end of the long, ordinary workday with the end of life's long day of toil. There is no saying that "this is compared with that," or that "this is a type or image of that." No, they are simply spoken of as one, as if you could not end your day's stint of labor except in the spirit with which you end the long stint of life itself.

Compline does not soften or attempt to rationalize the idea of death. When this life's work is over, you yield your spiritual component or soul to its Creator, just as each night you yield your sensitive psychic structure to the remoteness from daily reality that we call sleep. Death remains a punishment for the naturally guilt-laden human race. Also, in the whole course of the cosmos, death is the portal to new life. Through the New Life that divine death has made accessible for me, my individual death is likewise a portal through which I pass. If I have had the courage to accept life and all that the Creator does with me and for me during the course of each day of that life, if I have let Him *work with me*, let Him have His own peculiar and inexplicable way with me during this pilgrimage, I shall not be hopelessly perplexed when I come to the end of this term. The Amen of death will be simply the logical successor of all the Amens I have spoken throughout my entire life: Amens that I have spoken, because of my Creator's Amen in heaven, Amens that mean I am trying to walk with God.

Walking with God means that we stay close to Him in prayer, and the loneliness we may experience in old age should drive us to closer fellowship with Him, toward whose life and peace we are ever moving.

I am not proposing any particular devotional exercises. It will be ample if we preserve even a fraction of those to which we have accustomed ourselves during our life. But, simply, in all such matters we can act with more meaning, we can remember when we speak to God that we are not talking to one remote and strange, but to one who is more subjectively concerned with me than I am myself. "While man's problem is God, God's problem is man," as Rabbi Abraham J. Heschel so strikingly says, for "worship of God without justice to man is an abomination."[1] And he notes that "life is a response, not a soliloquy." It is He who is seeking the opportunity to enter into me, and to sit down

[1] A. J. Heschel, *God in Search of Man*, Meridian, Philadelphia, 1961, pp. 144, 238.

and converse with me: as Father, as a Brother, as the Spirit who is the guest of my own spirit, and lives within me.

Old age is the time of prayer, in this intimate and informal sense, the time of companionship or easy conversation. We become more and more actively conscious that we are not alone even as regards our fellow creatures, but are united with the great praying world of God's children. I pray with those who are of my faith, that our common faith may be to speak with the convincing voice of fellowship, the power of that congregation, our own Mother, which speaks to the most High as a bride to the bridegroom. The more I identify myself with that great company, the more readily will I forget the temporary accident of loneliness: indeed, I may come in a way to treasure that opportunity of great solitude, so that I may commune more readily with my own spiritual brothers and sisters. But when I have done so, I shall profit all the more by fellowship with those persons with whom I *can* converse in earthly fashion.

Moreover, we in old age should pray in a special manner as united with those who may be not of our faith, but who have faith, and who, too, pray to the Most High. These words, meaningful at any time are most meaningful today, when all men and women of faith, all men and women of reverence and moral integrity are threatened by the hordes that would destroy all reverence, all love, all the foundations of personality itself.

Old age, too, is the time when we need the *courage to love*. The courage, let us say, to think *more* of other people, rather than less; to go out of oneself, rather than to withdraw and close the curtains and brood.

On Charley Carmody's birthday, his 81st—which he puckishly insisted was his 82nd—his friends and relatives asked Charley to "give us your best advice." "And what d'ye think I tell them?" answered Mr. Carmody. "No smokin' or drinkin'? Go to bed by sunset? Don't eat fat? No! *I tell them, keep thinkin' of other people.* That's always been my rule and that's why I am happy today."

Well, that was a nice idea on Mr. Carmody's part, though his "thinking of other people" included his never-failing recollection of how much they owed him for unpaid rent. His love was not all pure benevolence.[2]

If we have the courage to walk with God in prayer, and if, like Charley Carmody, we keep thinking of other people—not to collect their rents, but to love them as God Himself made us to love them—we shall see something of the meaning of old age. But this means we must love people in their entirety, with their rough edges as well as their pleasant qualities.

To walk with God takes courage, and in old age God asks us to walk with Him. He asks us not to be frightened at what we see, or dismayed at what we hear, because He is with us, and knows from His own experience what life on this earth is, even though He Himself has not suffered the drawbacks of old age.

Two large mural paintings adorn, on opposite sides, the walls of the westernmost end of the nave of Trinity Church

[2] E. O'Connor, *The Edge of Sadness*, Little, Brown & Co., Boston, 1960, p. 78.

in Boston. They have a certain personal interest for me, and, whenever chance brings me to Boston and Copley Square, I am apt to visit them. They are poorly lighted, and the sexton needs to throw some switches in order to bring them into full view.

Each of these paintings is a lesson in courage: not physical prowess, but the courage that comes from the willingness to seek and publicly announced the truth.

The painting on your right, as you enter the church from the west, represents the courage of an inquiry, a dangerous inquiry under the political conditions that prevailed in Judea at the time the inquiry was made. Nicodemus believed in the Resurrection after death, because he was a Pharisee. He took it so seriously that he came by night to ask the great Teacher about the Kingdom of God, and the new life, that went with the Kingdom.

The Master's room is dimly lighted by a flickering olive-oil lamp. Fitfully, the mild breeze from the lake wafts in and out through the open window. "The wind breathes where it will," says the Master, taking a cue from the surroundings, "and thou canst hear the sound of it, but knowest nothing of the way it came or the way it goes: so it is, when a man is born by the breath of the Spirit." The free movement of the wind is a sign of the movement of the Spirit of God that has hovered over mankind from the beginning, that has spoken to every succeeding generation by the Prophets, in an ever more insistent declaration of the moral law the Creator has planted in our hearts, in cumulative references to the great consummation at the end of history. Now the Spirit has come to dwell in man, pro-

[131]

vided we freely invite His presence. He has come to create in each person who accepts the Spirit, who says Amen to his presence, the supreme gift of the new life of the Resurrection: a rebirth, a being "born again."

"How is it possible," asks Nicodemus, "that man should be born when he is already old?"

The Teacher mildly rebukes him. "Can such things seem strange to thee, who are one of the teachers of Israel?" At the same time, the Teacher drives home the essential point: that the new life is begun here in Baptism, in the symbolical "dying" by water raised to sacramental power by the Holy Spirit. Yet through this baptismal death we rise even now to the life that will be revealed to us after death. This is the meaning which Nicodemus is seeking, and he has the courage to receive and to accept it.

The Samaritan woman's inquiry, pictured in the painting opposite, is of a different character. Her question concerns the living water, the water of life, that the Teacher describes to her in vivid terms and which is at his disposal.

She has the courage to ask questions of him point-blank, right in the face of his shattering exposition of her disordered personal conduct. Moreover, she is brave enough to announce his answer to her townfolk, and to urge them, too, to hurry out of the town and invite Him to come and stay with them.

Of totally different character and background from Nicodemus, she is one with the learned and pious Pharisee in her frank insistence upon seeking the gift of eternal life. Like Nicodemus, she is not dismayed by the discovery that the life which is given *now* in obscurity and humility will be realized and enjoyed in the world to come.

About the woman at the well there is no further history, except that she apparently came back for more information. Of Nicodemus, however, we have the record that he had the courage to face up to the dissident elements among his own religious associates; to identify himself at the supreme moment with the despised and rejected Teacher, this time at grave personal risk. When Joseph of Arimathea came to the hill of Golgotha to take away the body of the crucified Jesus, with him was Nicodemus, "the same who made his first visit to Jesus by night."

The life of the Resurrection — in its present hidden form, in its expected glory — had challenged the faith and the courage of these two most disparate people, the cautiously courageous man, the boldly courageous woman. As long as we live, life presents this challenge of courage to the old. Death will, as it were, take care of itself, if we but use reasonable diligence now to put our house in order, if we talk often to Him whom we are one day to meet face to face, if we remember His love for us.

When you are old, when you are approaching the end of life's journey, it would seem to be the most natural thing to talk of death. If the family is going abroad for the summer, especially if it's for the first time, conversation for months ahead is taken up with places to visit, preparations for the journey, friends or relatives to be greeted.

Since death is the entrance into that life for which we are made, which is the sum of all our expectations and hopes, it would seem very strange if we should not be anxious to talk about it. The fact that we know so little as to just how the transition takes place, would seem to be an argument that we should be all the more eager to discuss the little knowledge we do possess. We would want to piece together the sum of our intuitions and experiences. The fact that this transition affects us all without exception, whatsoever, is an added reason why we should be interested in such a unique and wonderful event. Nobody, no matter what distractions one may build up, can escape the thought of death. Then why not talk of it?

It is curious that our customs and folklore seem to conspire against such a type of conversation. The most fearful, the really most interesting topic in the world is banned in polite conversation. Our slice-of-life periodicals, our communications media of all sorts will feature every kind of death-dealing violence: corpses, funerals, and tombs, but they are very reluctant to discuss the simple act of life's termination.

Lavishly we spend time and money elaborating funerals and obituaries. Funeral services themselves, with the chanting of the *Dies Irae* and other admonitions to lead a better life, feature death as a platform for pious exhortation. Other funeral rites try to erase the stark fact of death from our consciousness, by appropriate music, selected hymns and psalms, not to speak of floral offerings. As for the obituaries, it is curious that you have to wait until a fairly prominent person has departed in order to get a good, well-written account of his or her life, the notice from the local paper that for some years past has been set up in type, with room for minor corrections and additions.

Courage in Old Age

The early Christians, from what I have been able to gather, do not seem to have suffered any great inhibitions against talking about death, even when it was not a question of martyrdom. Their tombs and inscriptions give the impression of a quite cheerful familiarity: reverence for death, but not gloomy anxiety.

I do not find anything in our faith, as I know it, to encourage a diffident attitude. The sting of death, says St. Paul, is sin. Yet by our sacramental baptism we are freed from the sin of our first parents, with its sentence of exile from our true home. The sacrament of Penance — or "confession," humble and frank — frees us from the chains of our personal wrongdoing. The first action of a priest called to minister to the dying is to bring to them this blessed "setting-free," this liberation, whatever may have been the score up to now. Why should we be frightened at the idea of obtaining such a liberation? We certainly spend enough hours in discussing the ways and means the doctors and hospitals provide for freeing us from physical pains. If we talk habitually of death, as a natural phenomenon, we would not be acting like some of our good (and I emphasize the *good*, it can go high in the scale of goodness) Catholic people who seem to think that it augurs disaster if the sacramental offices of our Church are called into service one minute before the latest possible opportunity.

Certainly we shall need courage in the last moments of our lives. Whatever the experience may actually be, everyone seems agreed that the collapse of our life-forces is part of the final working-out of our time-existence. Yet the Church's sacramental anointing is expressly given in order to strengthen and integrate us in this moment; to effect, in ways that we can never fully anticipate, the strengthening, calming, reassuring of that mysterious psychic realm, where body and soul meet, where the triumphant power of God's grace confronts the confusing powers of darkness. It is no mere chance that the chrism itself, by which the sick are anointed, is blessed by the Bishop at the high altar of the Cathedral on the solemn day, Holy Thursday, when the Church commemorates the opening scene in the final act of the great drama of the Redemption and Resurrection.

St. Augustine says that nobody should depart this life except in a spirit of penance. But penance and loving confidence are not opposites. Rather they are two sides to the same coin. Both are expressions of the simple and humble soul.

In the phenomenon of death, we are drawn into fellowship with all humanity, with all creation. As Fr. Teilhard de Chardin has so masterfully pointed out, in his *The Human Phenomenon*, we are steadfastly drawn into companionship with the development of the entire cosmos. In her sacramental ministrations, the Church draws us more closely than ever into her fellowship. All that the Church has is ours, as never before. The gift of the Viaticum, the sacramental Body and Blood of the Saviour, in that last hour (that "last" of the Last Sacraments), is a gift of perfect thanksgiving: the Lord giving thanks within us for the infinitely precious gift of life itself.

When we leave, our final and most solemn act is simply and humbly to thank Him for that gift, which itself is the meaning of old age, and to regret that we have not used it better.

Why, then, should we hesitate to talk of these things? Isn't it better to discuss them frequently, to clarify our thoughts, to rid ourselves of false fears, to settle upon those points that are essential? And we all profit by one another's experiences.

If by chance death comes suddenly and unannounced — and who can be sure that it won't — it will not then find us unprepared. If its approach is gradual, if we have learned to "die a little" as well as to "live a little," it will come as a friend. Our own terminal Amen will ring true as the response to the Creator's primal Amen which sent us into this world. In all penitence and contrition for our failings, we will say, like St. Patrick's *Grazagham,* "thanks be to God," for the gift of the golden bowl of life.

L.D.S.

18